CLASSIC ROCK BASS LINES

Transcribed by Steve Gorenberg

Cherry Lane Music Company
Director of Publications/Project Editor: Mark Phillips

ISBN 1-57560-777-8

Copyright © 2005 Cherry Lane Music Company
International Copyright Secured   All Rights Reserved

The music, text, design and graphics in this publication are protected by copyright law. Any duplication or transmission, by any means, electronic, mechanical, photocopying, recording or otherwise, is an infringement of copyright.

Visit our website at www.cherrylane.com

CONTENTS

3	Are You Gonna Go My Way	Lenny Kravitz
6	Birdland	Weather Report
15	Cat Scratch Fever	Ted Nugent
19	Crazy on You	Heart
23	Cut the Cake	Average White Band
28	Dixie Chicken	Little Feat
32	Don't Stop Believin'	Journey
37	Fairies Wear Boots	Black Sabbath
43	Feels Like the First Time	Foreigner
47	FM	Steely Dan
52	Getting Better	The Beatles
56	I Want You Back	Jackson 5
59	Lowdown	Boz Scaggs
62	Message in a Bottle	The Police
66	Minute by Minute	Doobie Brothers
70	My Generation	The Who
74	Rock & Roll - Part II	Gary Glitter
77	Rosanna	Toto
82	Roundabout	Yes
90	Satch Boogie	Joe Satriani
94	The Stroke	Billy Squier
96	Sunday Papers	Joe Jackson
103	Welcome to the Jungle	Guns N' Roses
107	What Is Hip	Tower of Power
112	You Can Call Me Al	Paul Simon
117	*Bass Notation Legend*	

ARE YOU GONNA GO MY WAY

Words by Lenny Kravitz
Music by Lenny Kravitz and Craig Ross

Copyright © 1993 Miss Bessie Music (ASCAP) and Wigged Music (BMI)
International Copyright Secured   All Rights Reserved

BIRDLAND

Music by Josef Zawinul

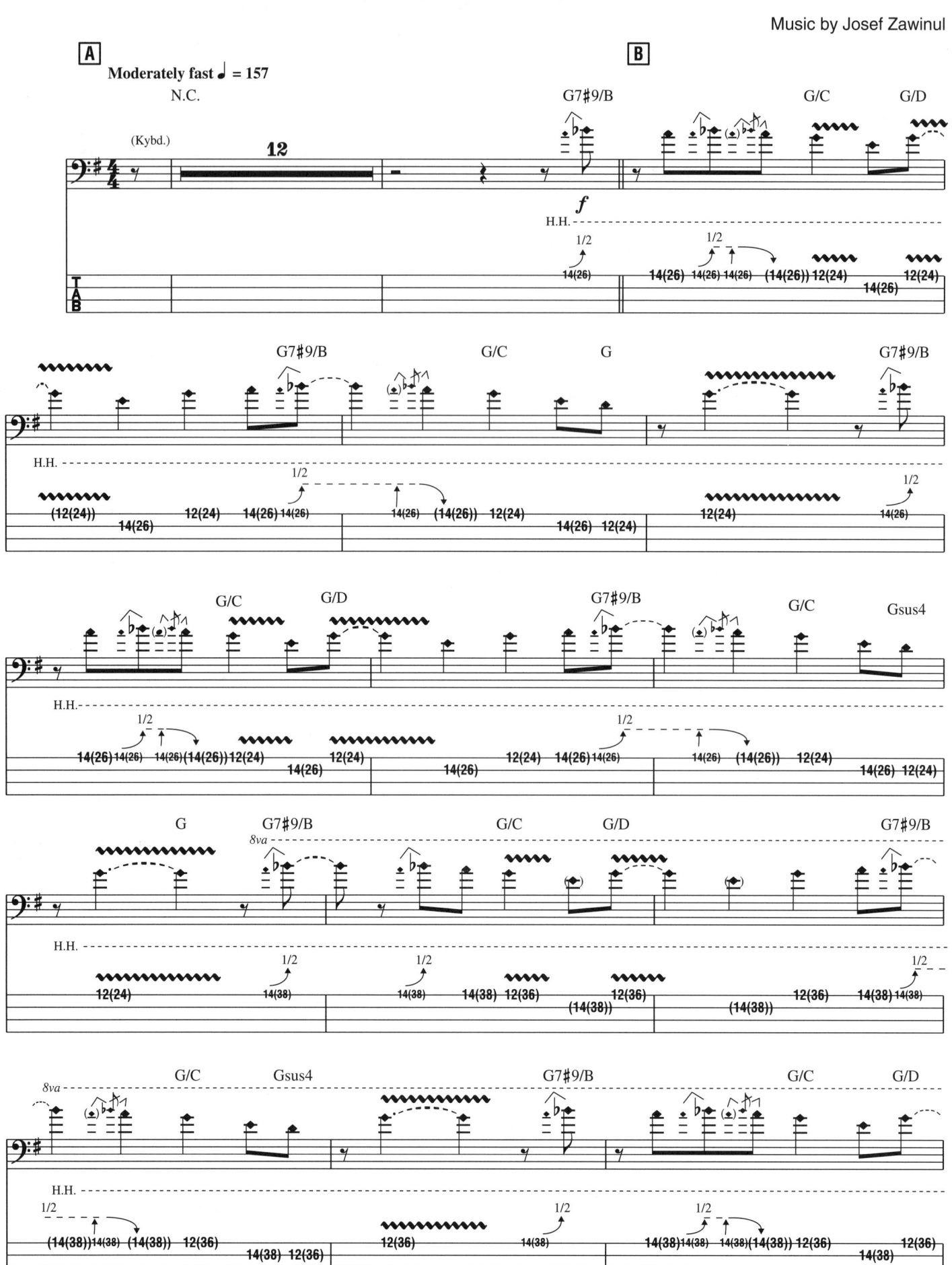

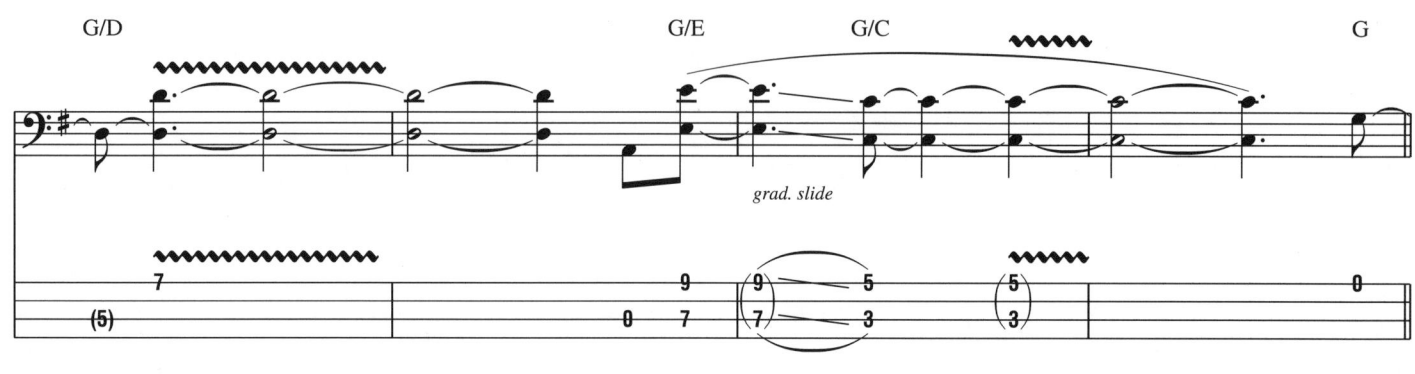
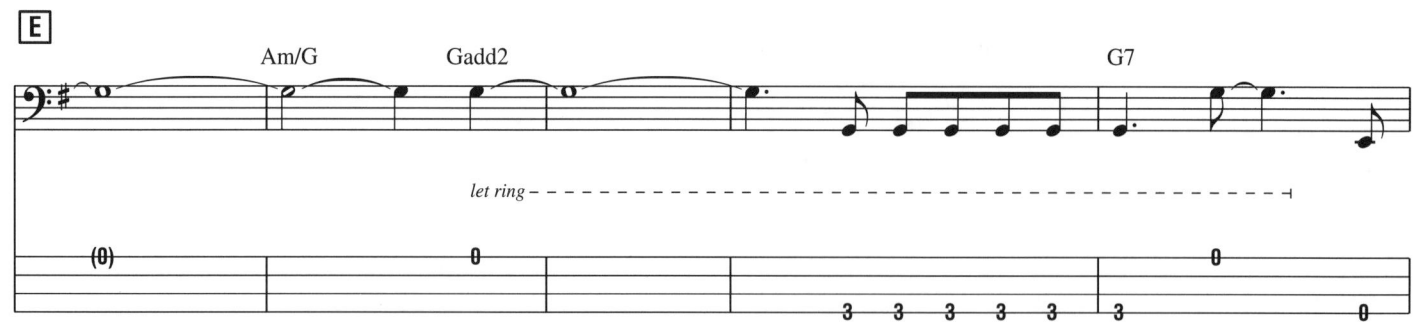
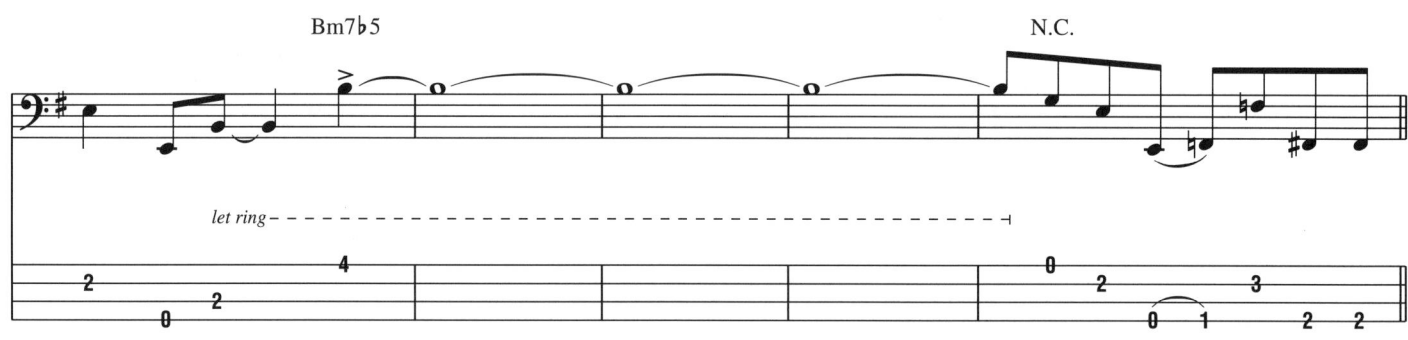
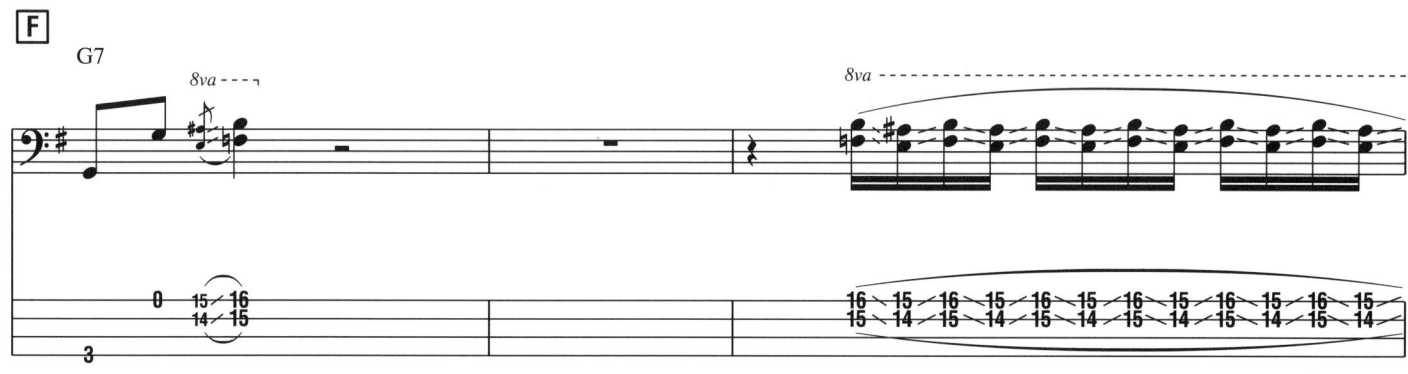

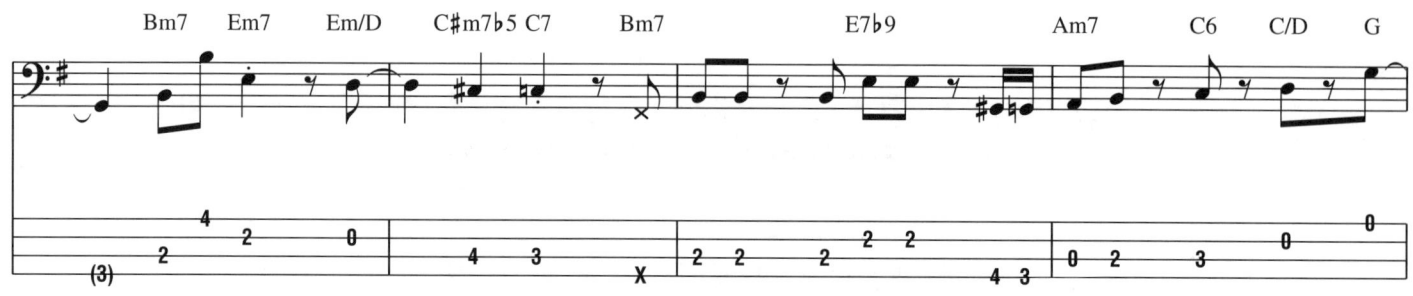
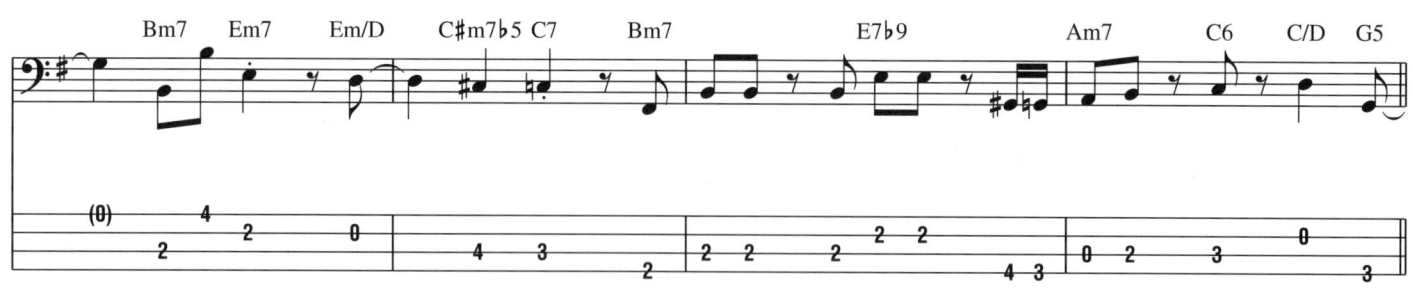

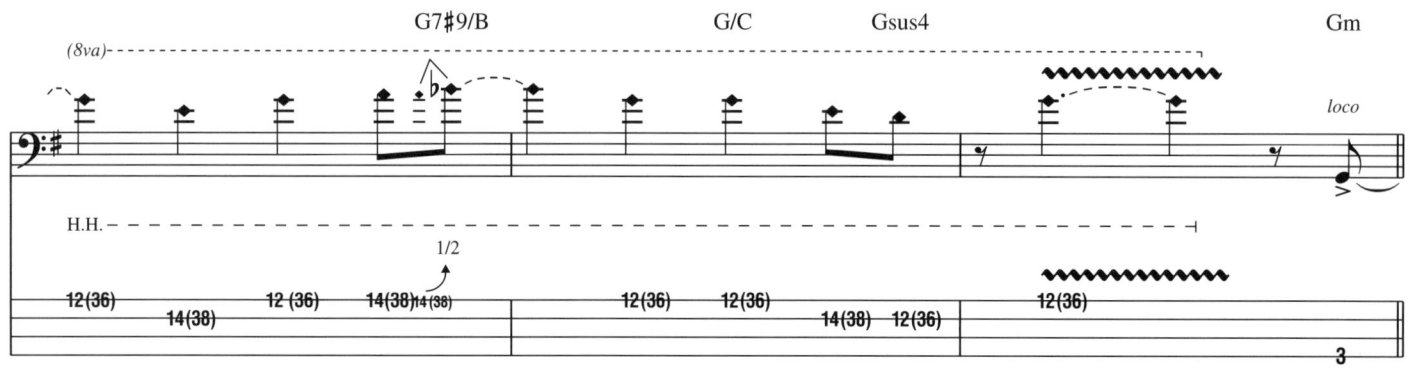
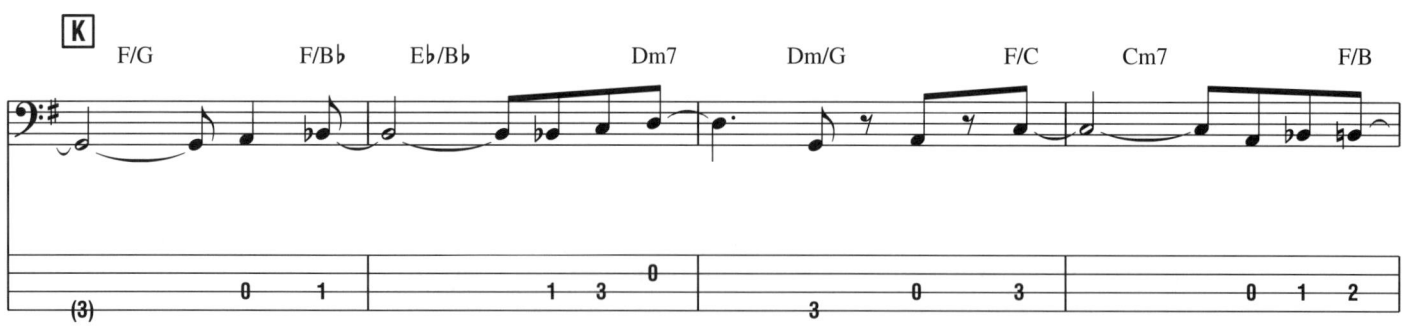
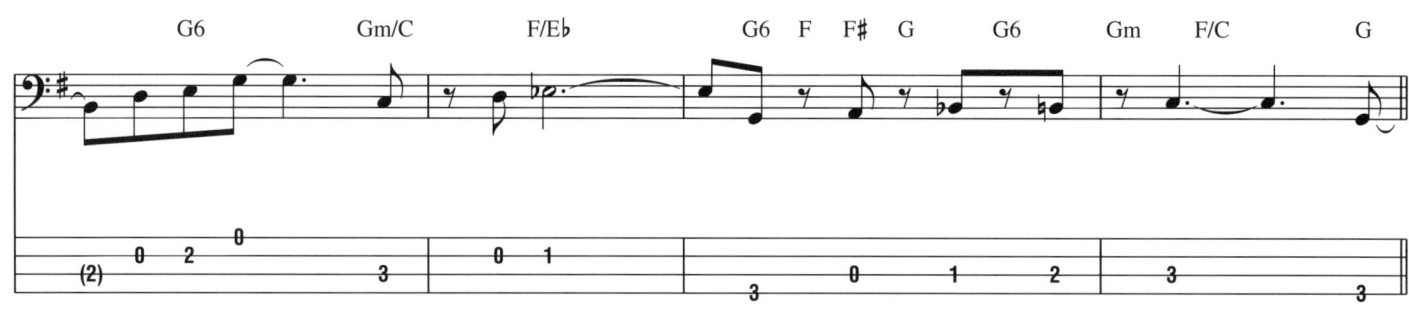
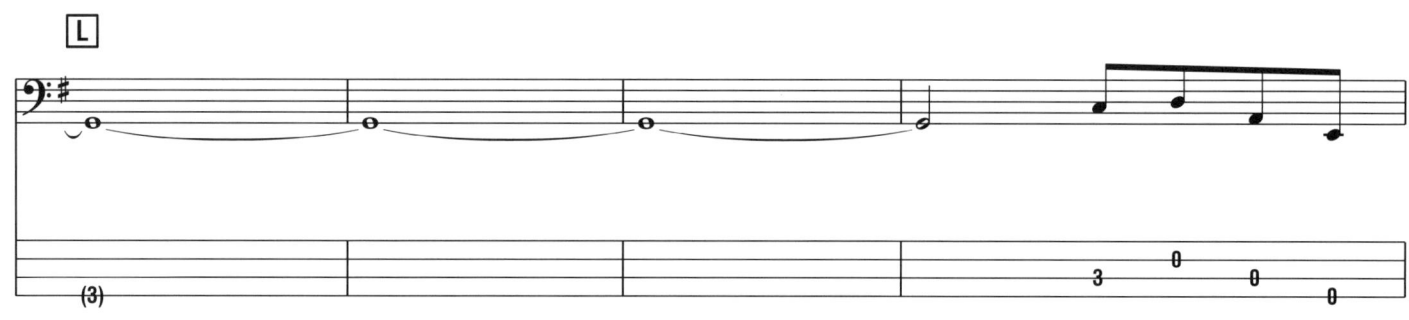
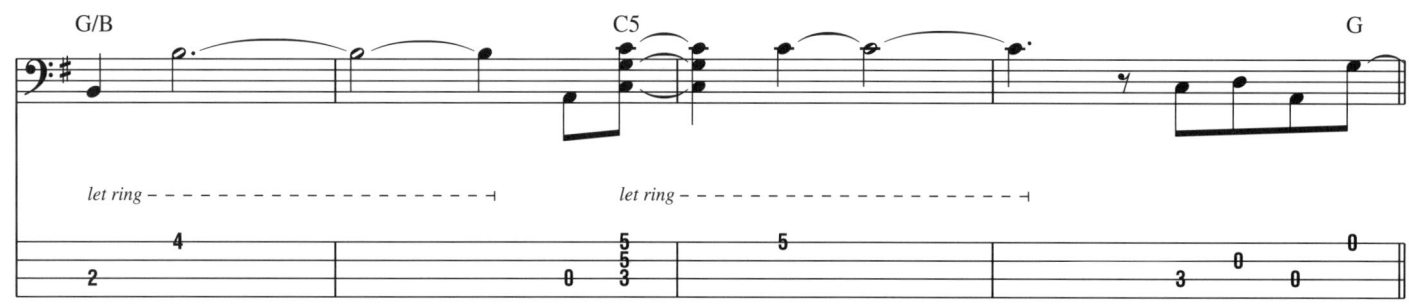

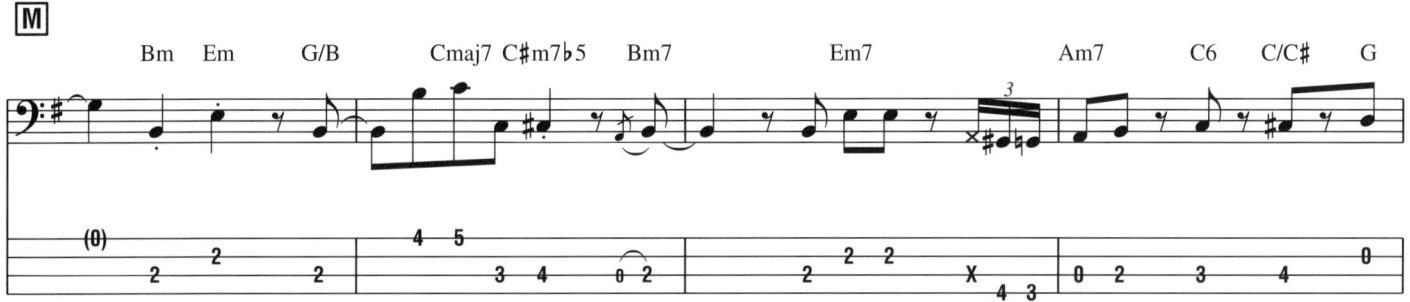
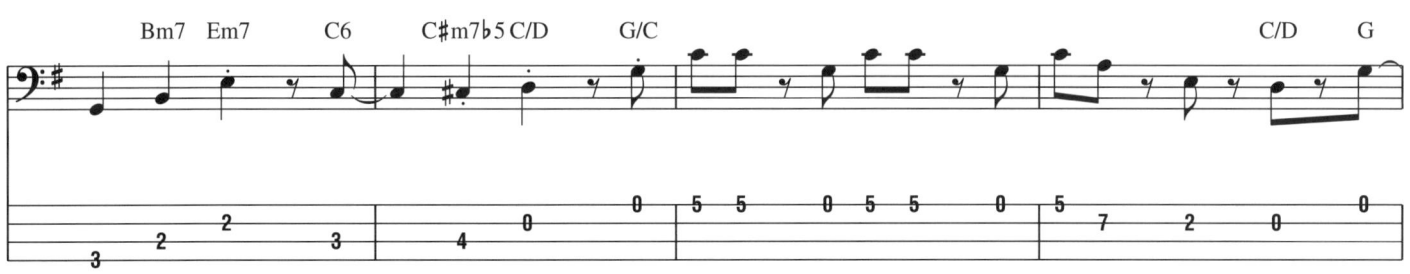
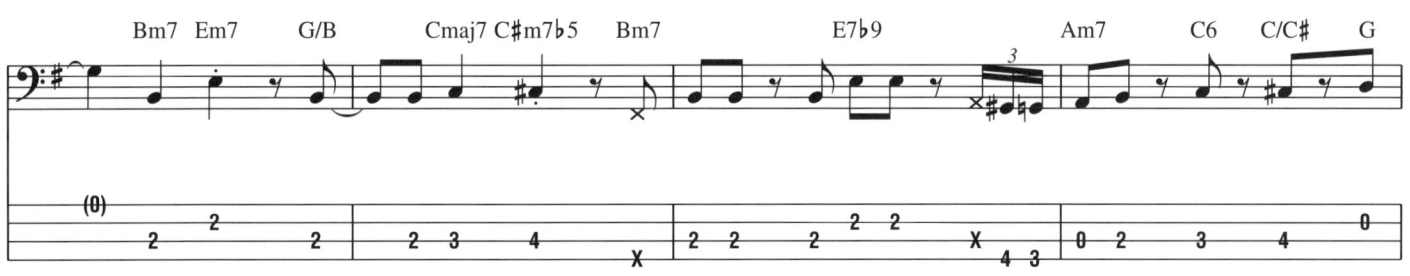
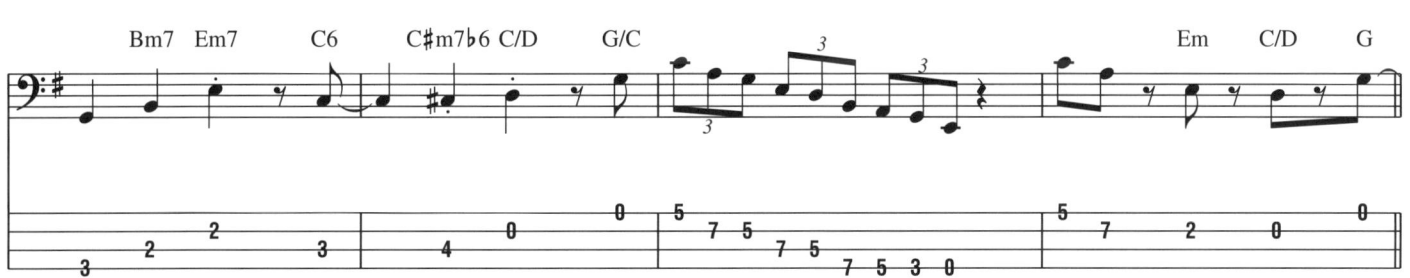

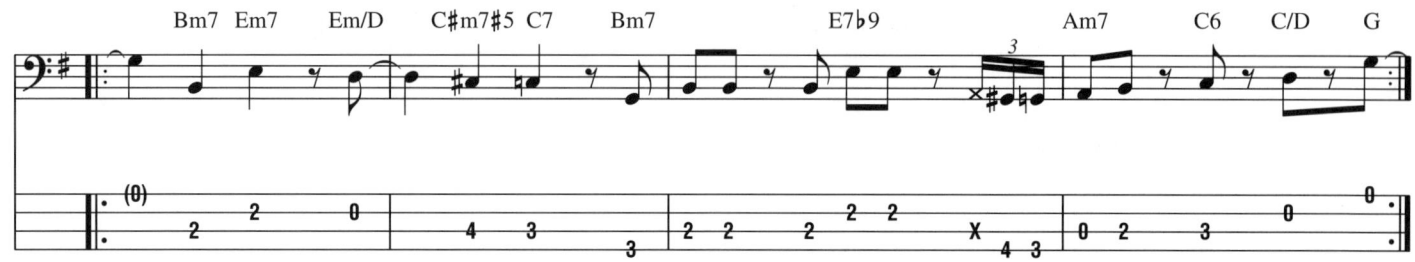

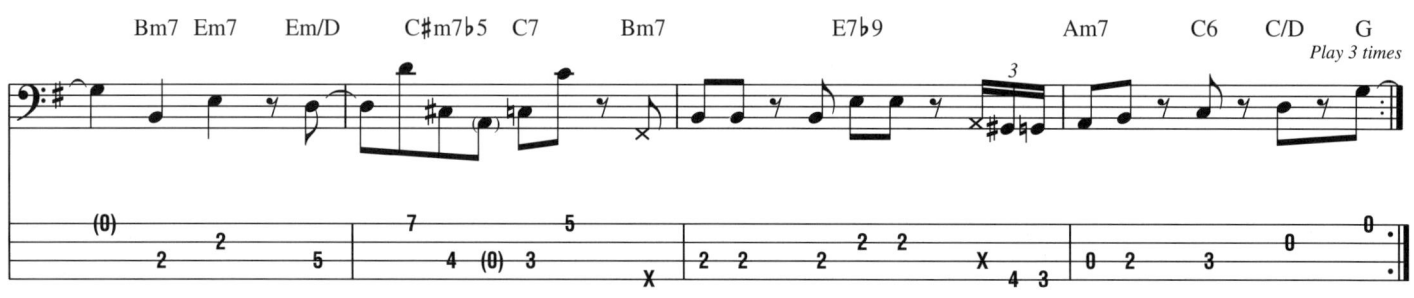

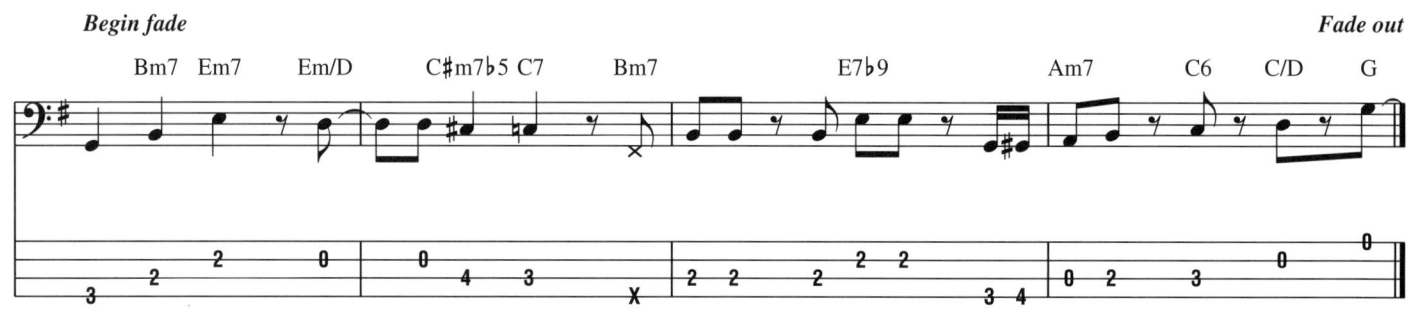

CAT SCRATCH FEVER

Words and Music by
Ted Nugent

Copyright © 1977 by Magicland Music
All Rights Reserved Used by Permission

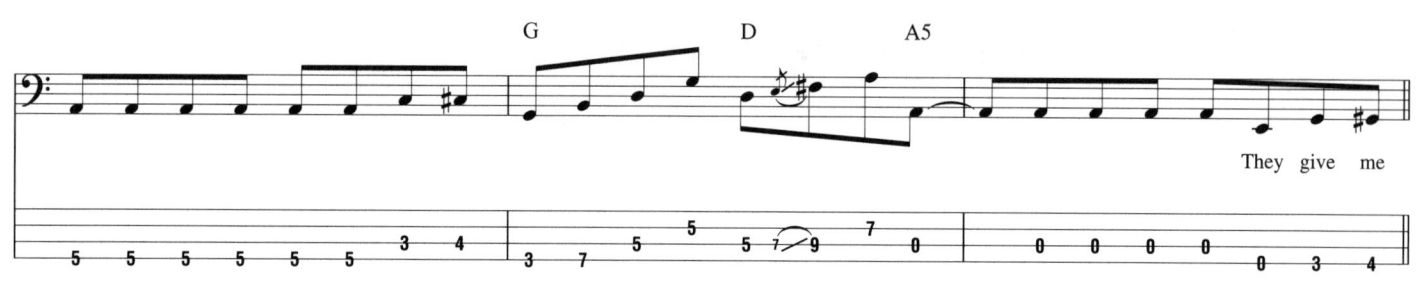

Chorus

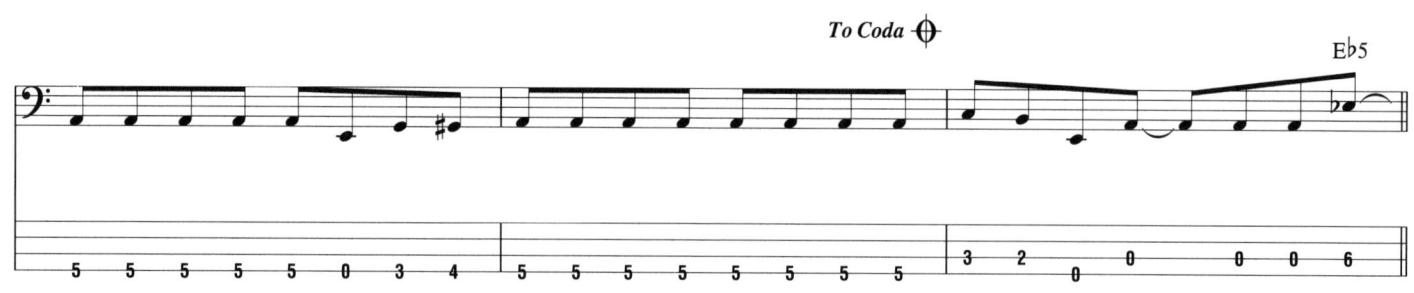

Bridge

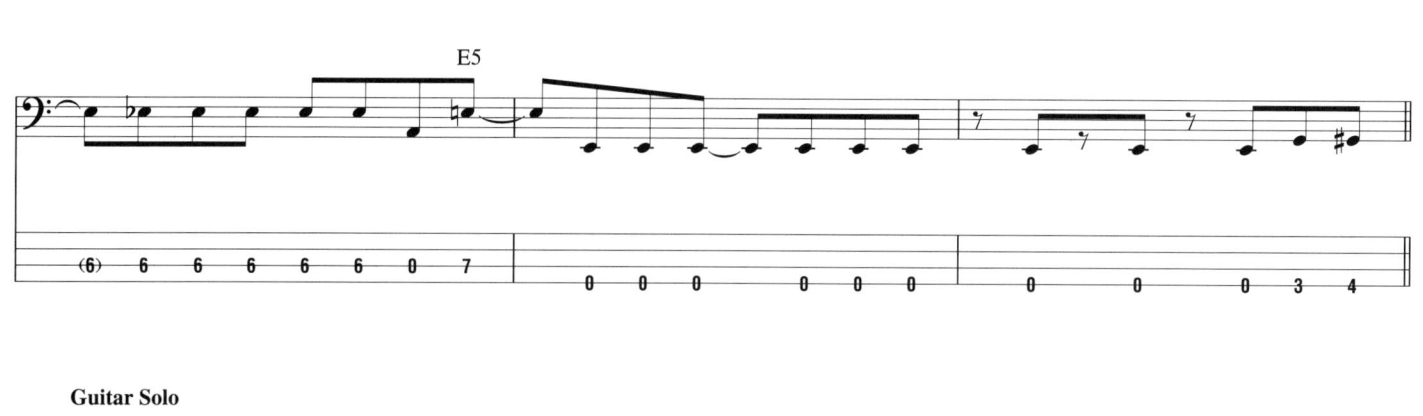

Guitar Solo

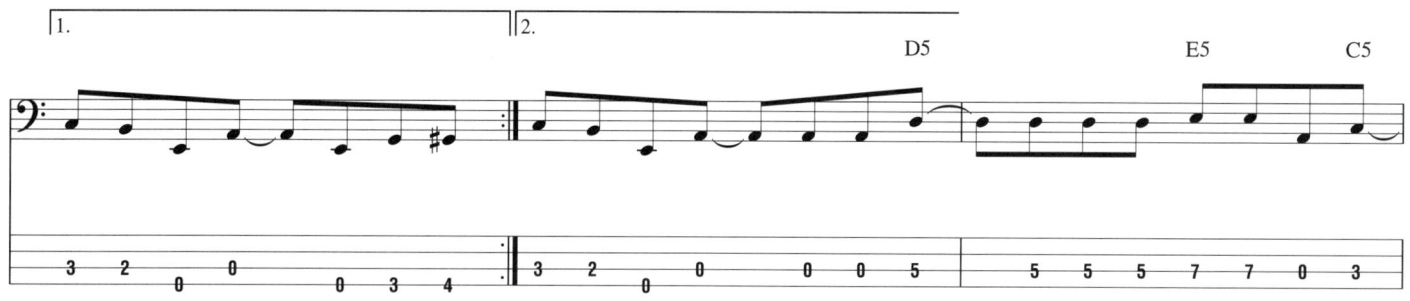

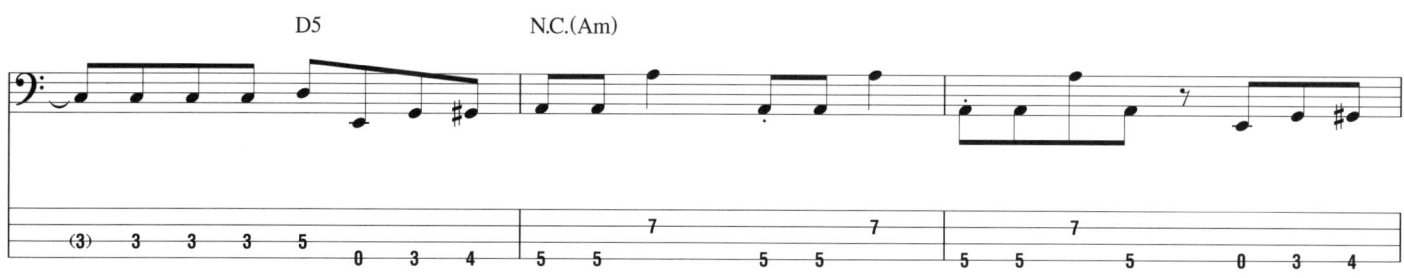

D.S. al Coda (take 2nd ending)

3. Well, I make

Coda

Breakdown

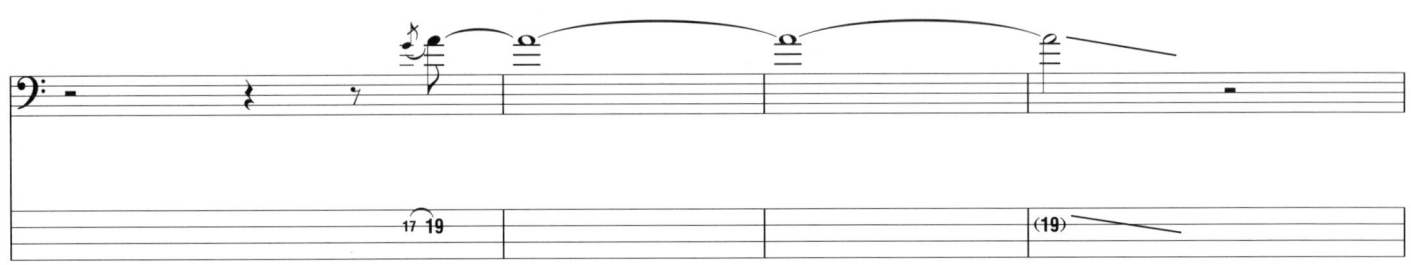

Chorus
N.C.(Am)

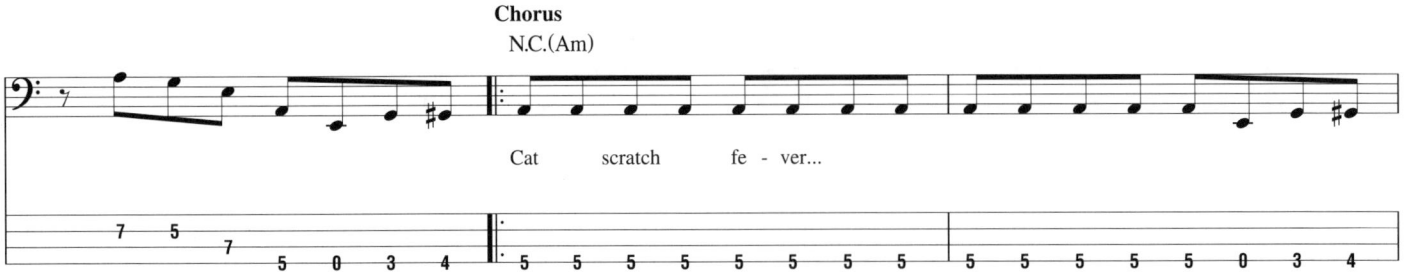

Cat scratch fe - ver...

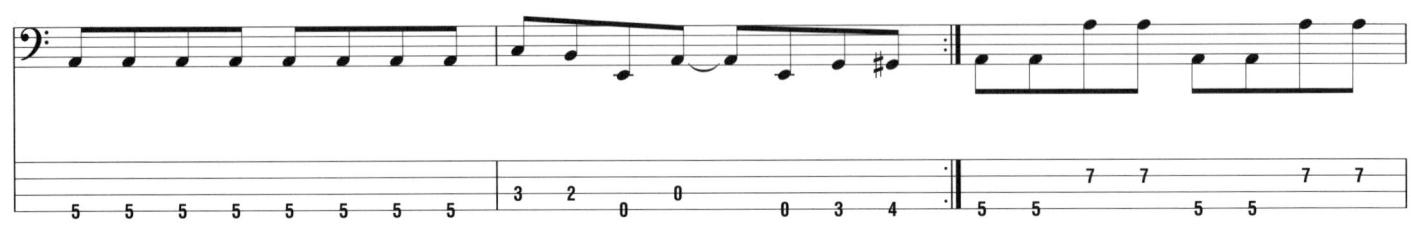

Outro
Free time

CRAZY ON YOU

Words and Music by
Ann Wilson, Nancy Wilson
and Roger Fisher

CUT THE CAKE

Written by James Stuart, Alan Gorrie,
Roger Ball and Owen McIntyre

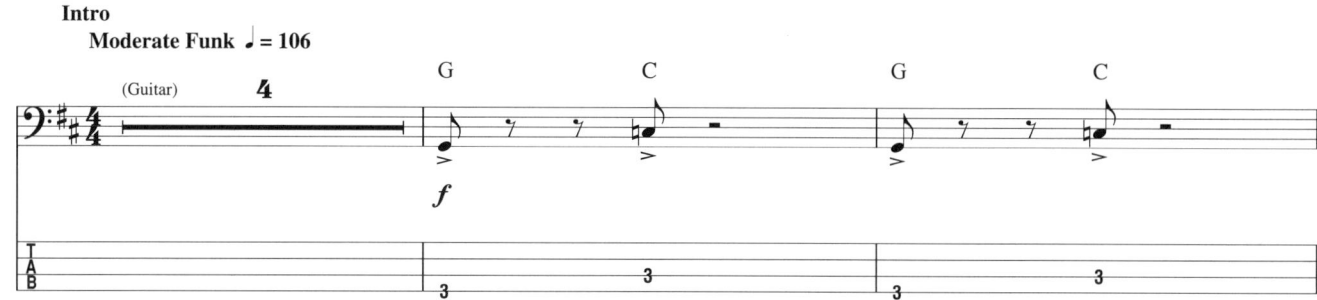

© 1975 (Renewed 2003) AVERAGE MUSIC (ASCAP)/Administered by BUG MUSIC, JOE'S SONGS, INC. (ASCAP) and FAIRWOOD MUSIC (PRS)
All Rights Reserved   Used by Permission

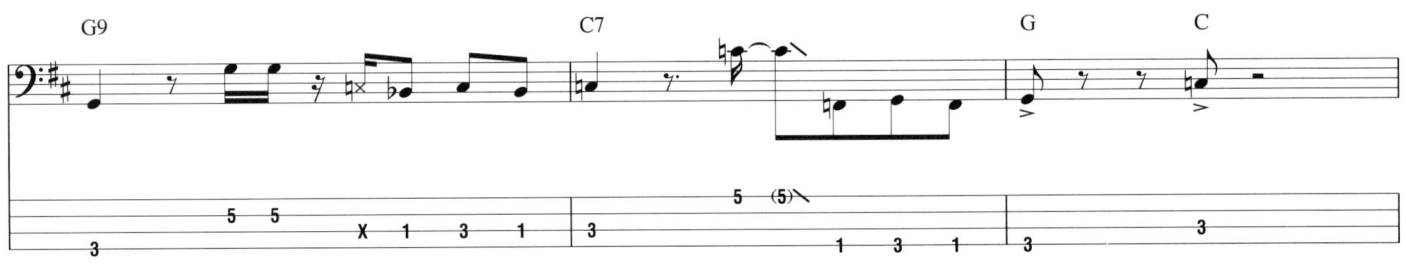

24

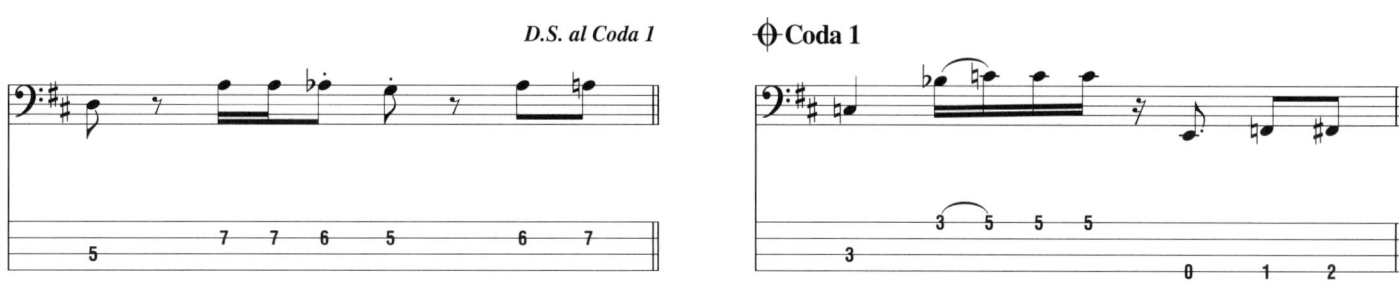

Chorus

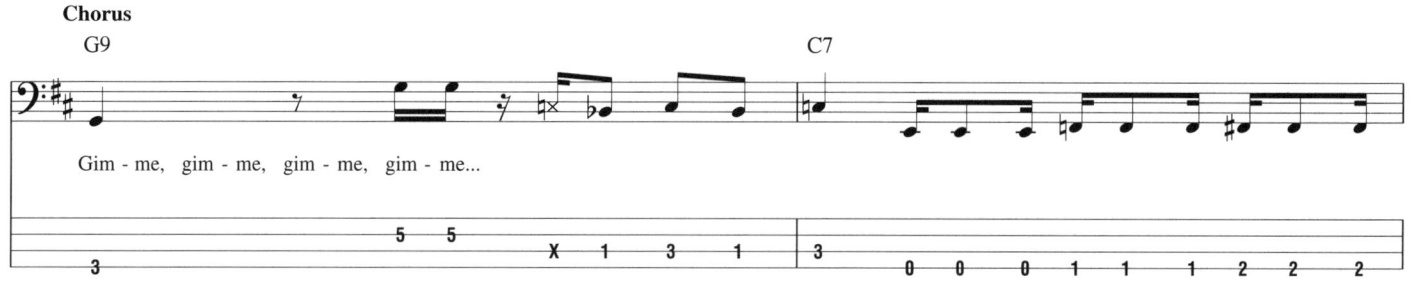

Gim - me, gim - me, gim - me, gim - me...

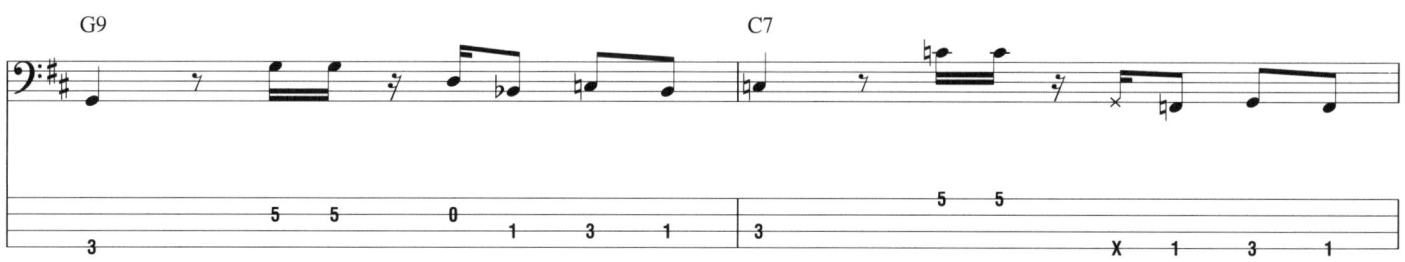

Breakdown

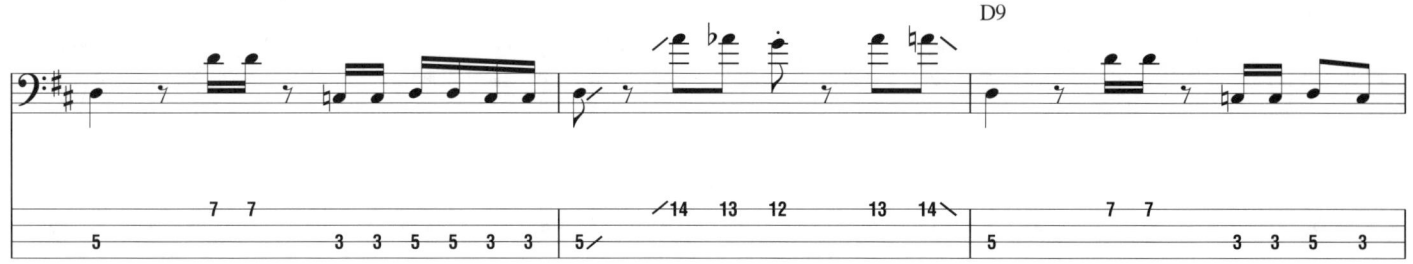

D.S. al Coda 2 Coda 2

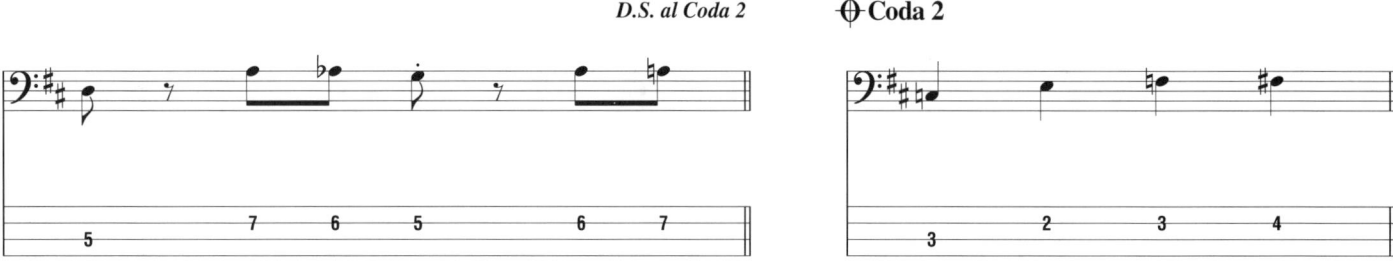

Chorus

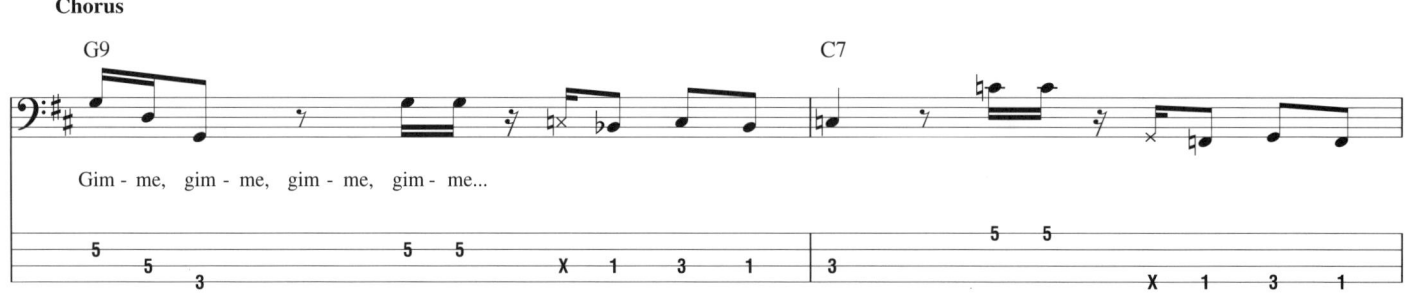

Gim - me, gim - me, gim - me, gim - me...

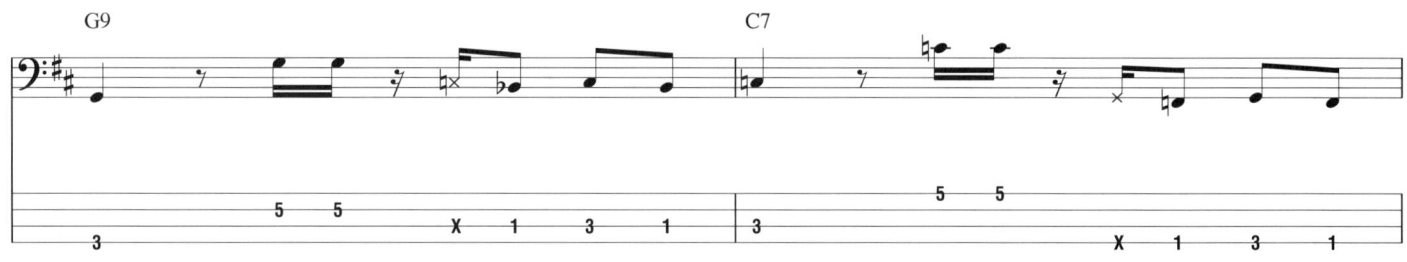

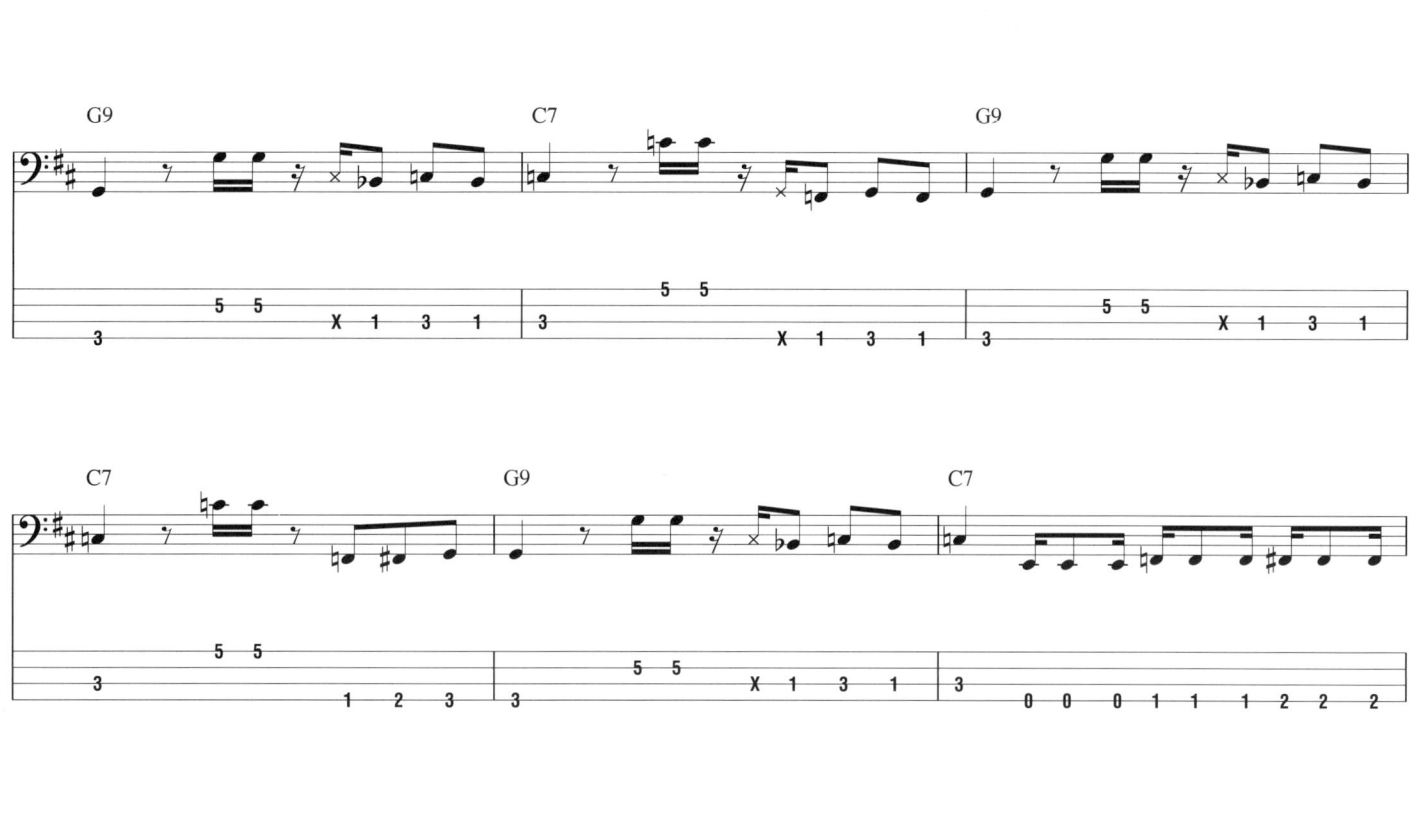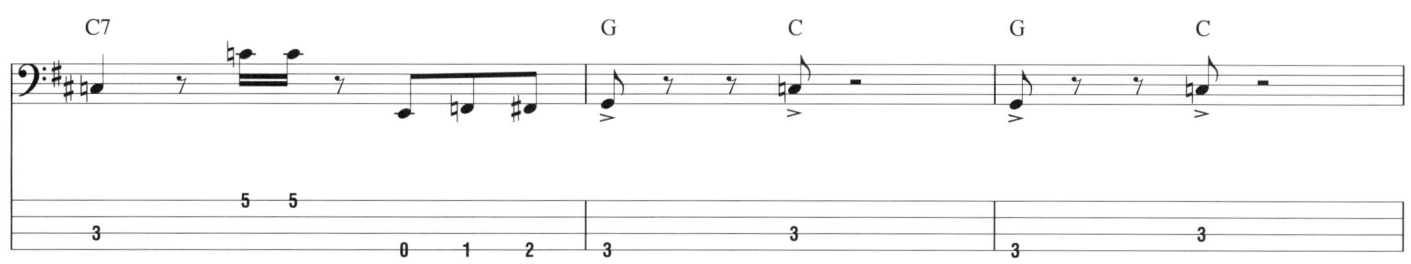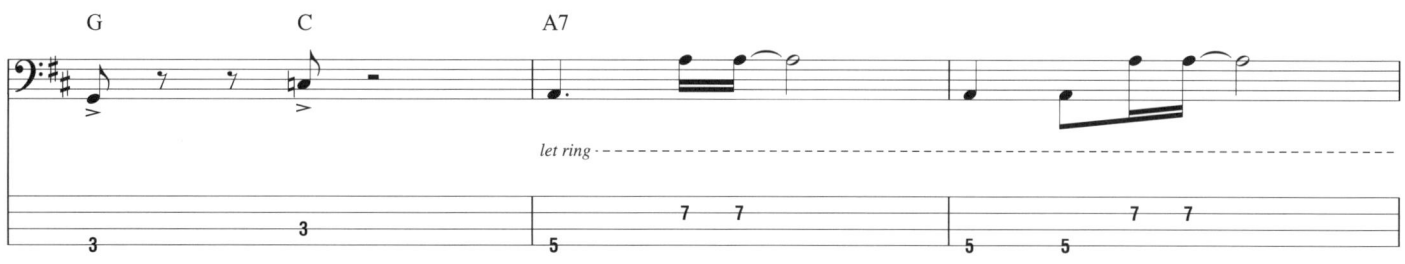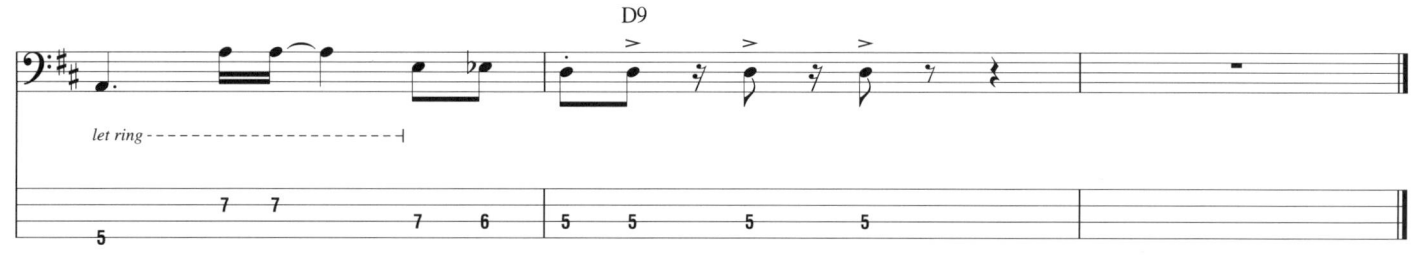

DIXIE CHICKEN

Words and Music by
Lowell George and Martin Kibbee

28

Copyright © 1973 (Renewed) Naked Snake Music (ASCAP)
All Rights Reserved

Yeah, well,

we made all the hot spots...

If you

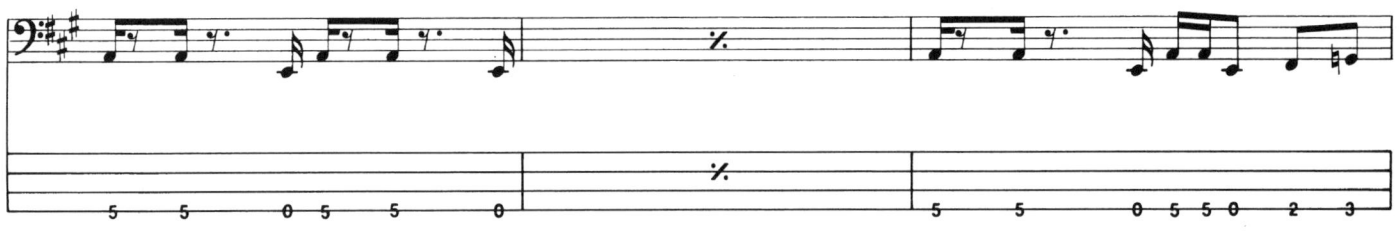

DON'T STOP BELIEVIN'

Words and Music by
Steve Perry, Neal Schon
and Jonathan Cain

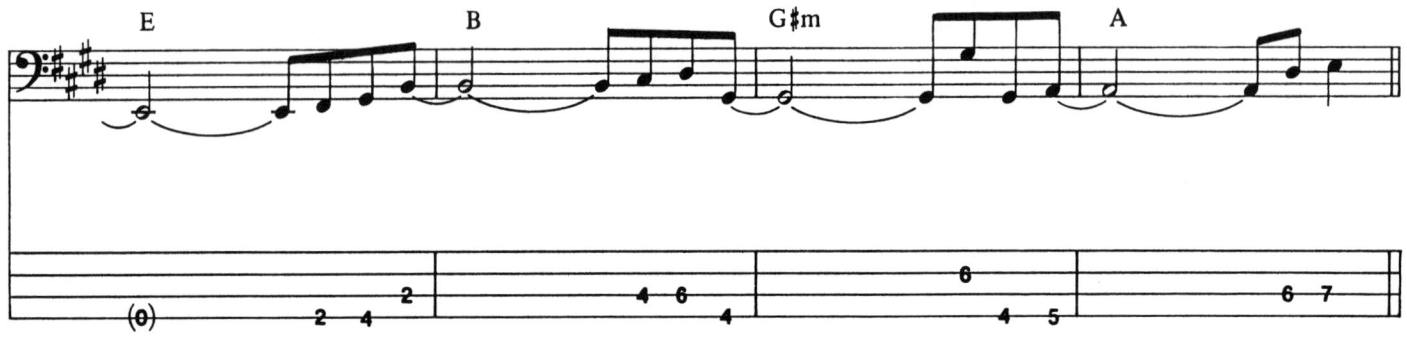
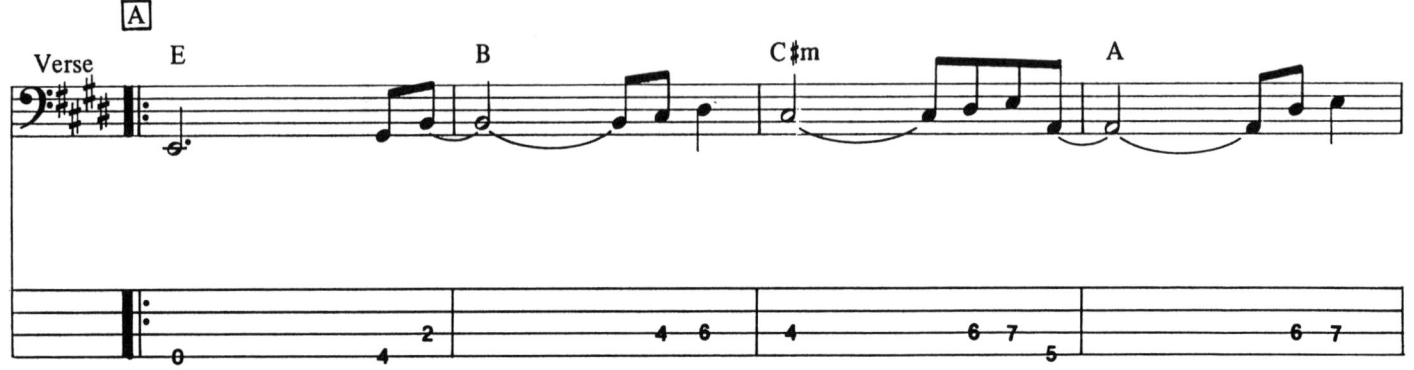

Copyright © 1981 Lacey Boulevard Music (BMI) and Weed High Nightmare Music (BMI)
International Copyright Secured   All Rights Reserved

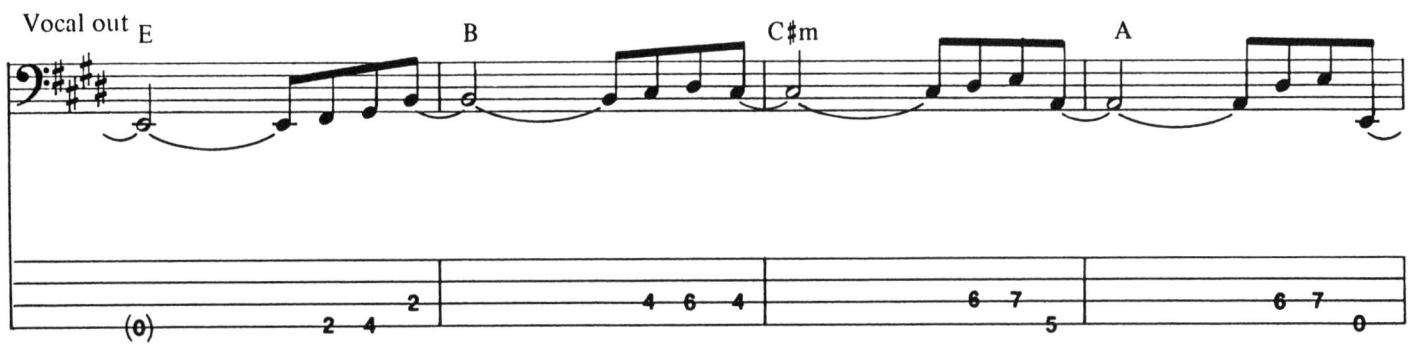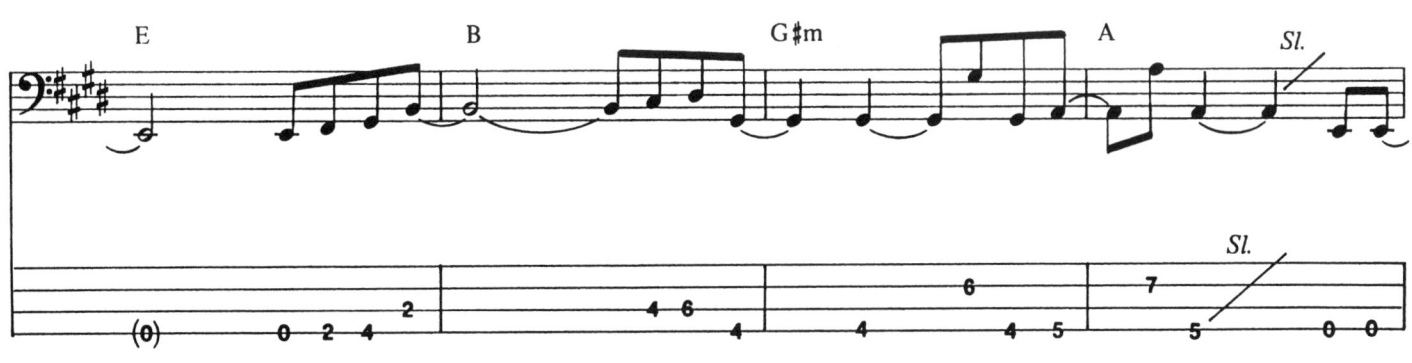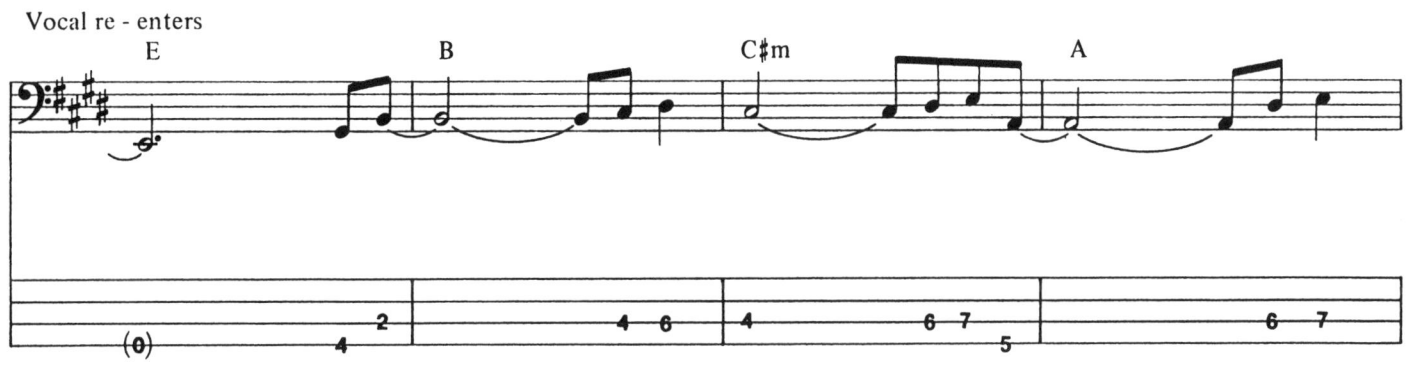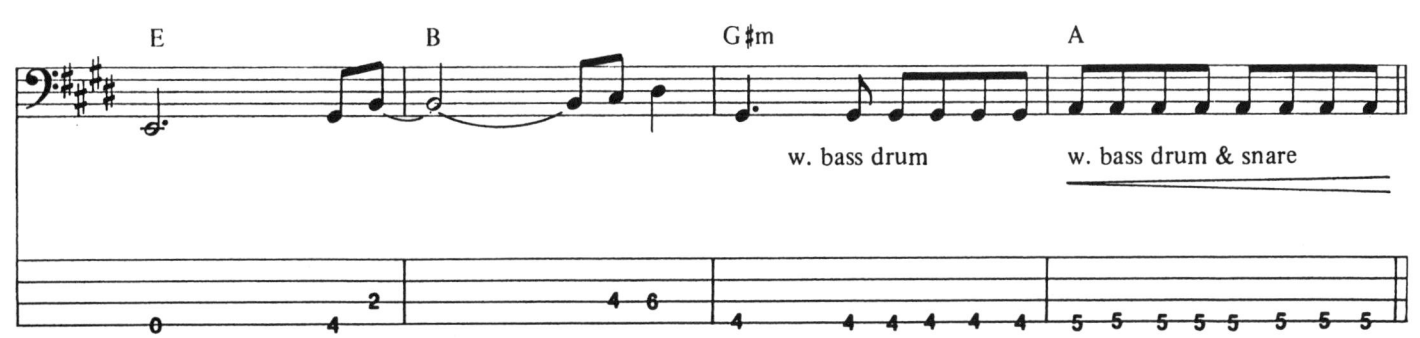

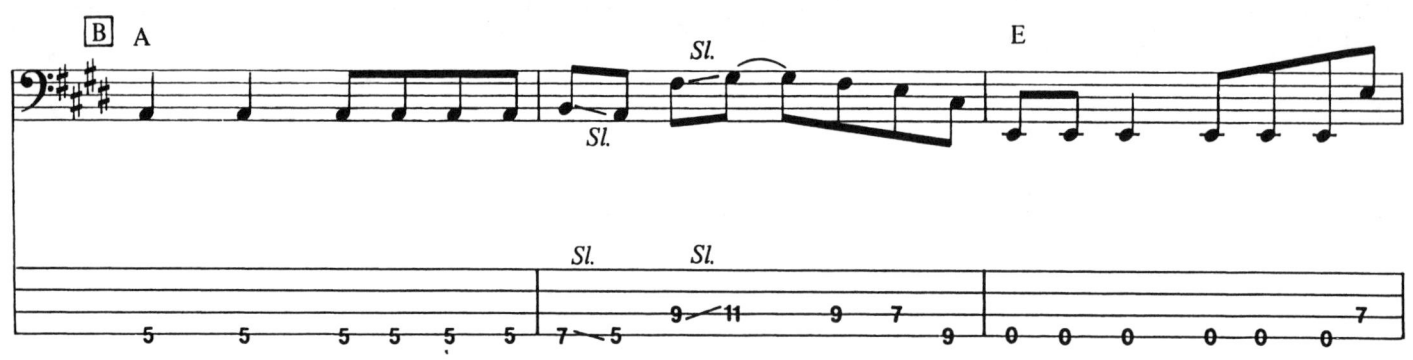
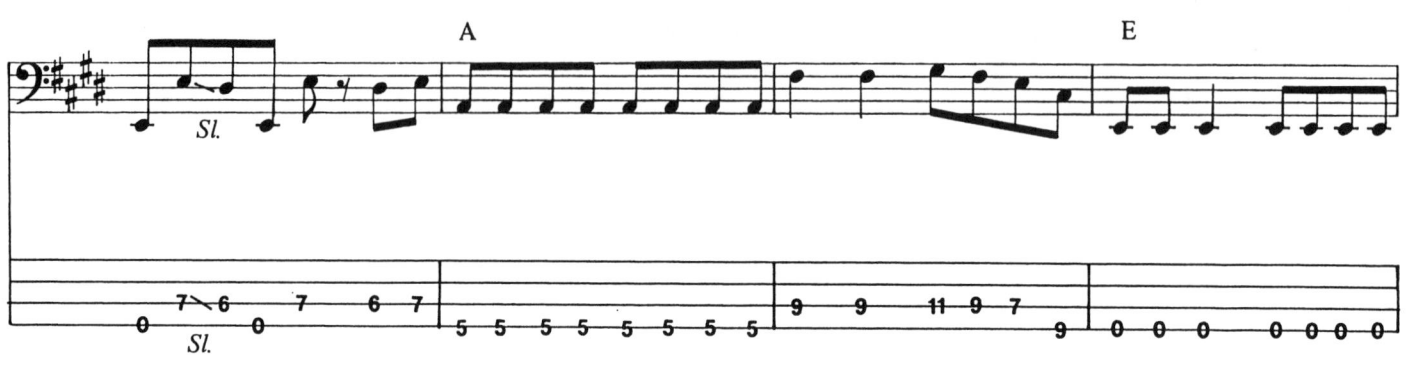
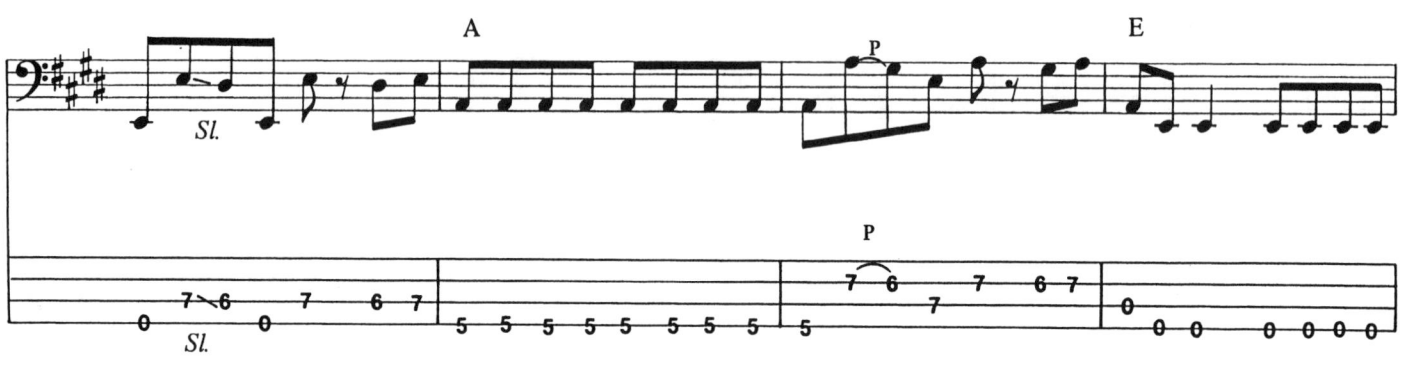
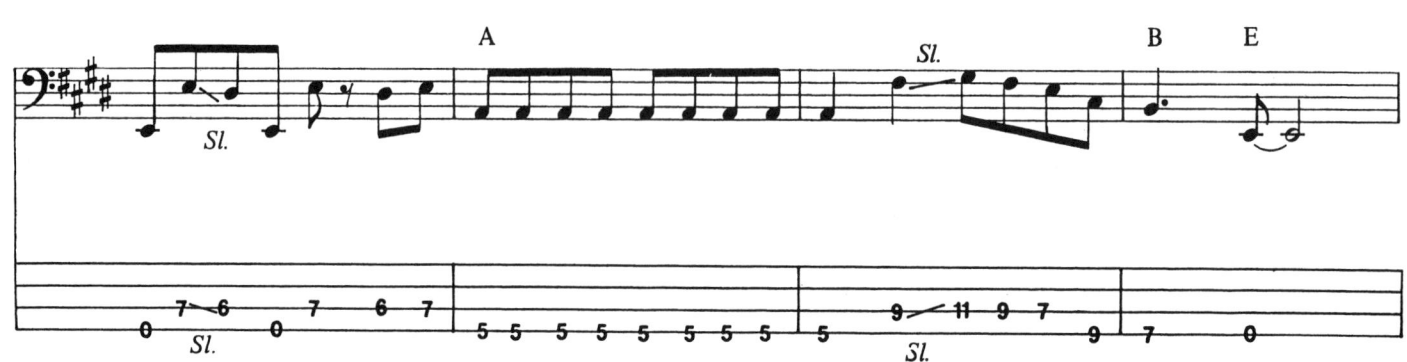

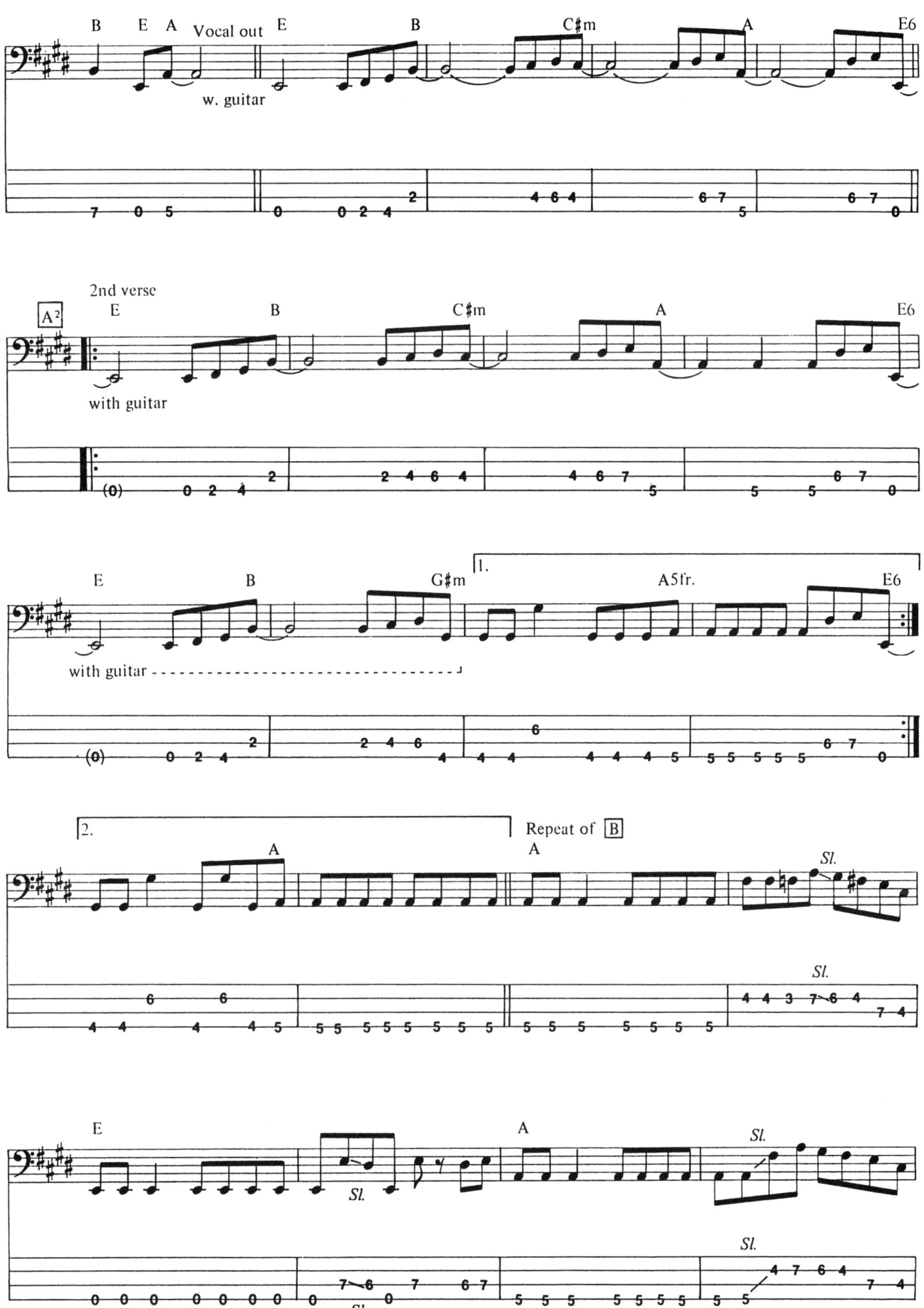

FAIRIES WEAR BOOTS
(Interpolating Jack the Stripper)

Words and Music by
Frank Iommi, John Osbourne,
William Ward and Terence Butler

"Jack the Stripper"
Moderately slow ♩ = 76

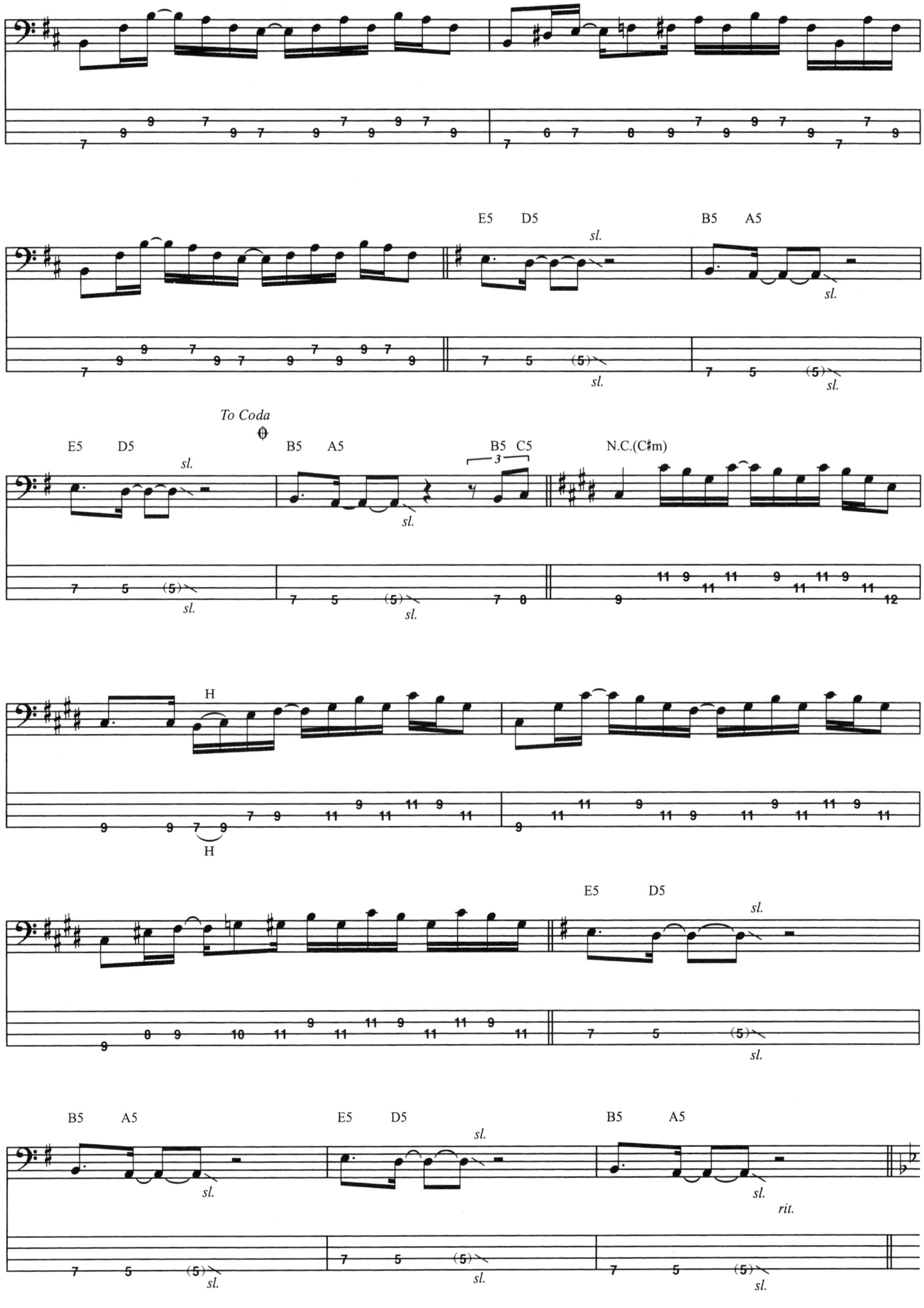
E5 D5
sl.
B5 A5
To Coda
B5 A5
B5 C5
N.C.(C♯m)
H
E5 D5
B5 A5
E5 D5
B5 A5
rit.

"Fairies Wear Boots"
Moderately ♩ = 124 (♫ = ♩ ♪ triplet)

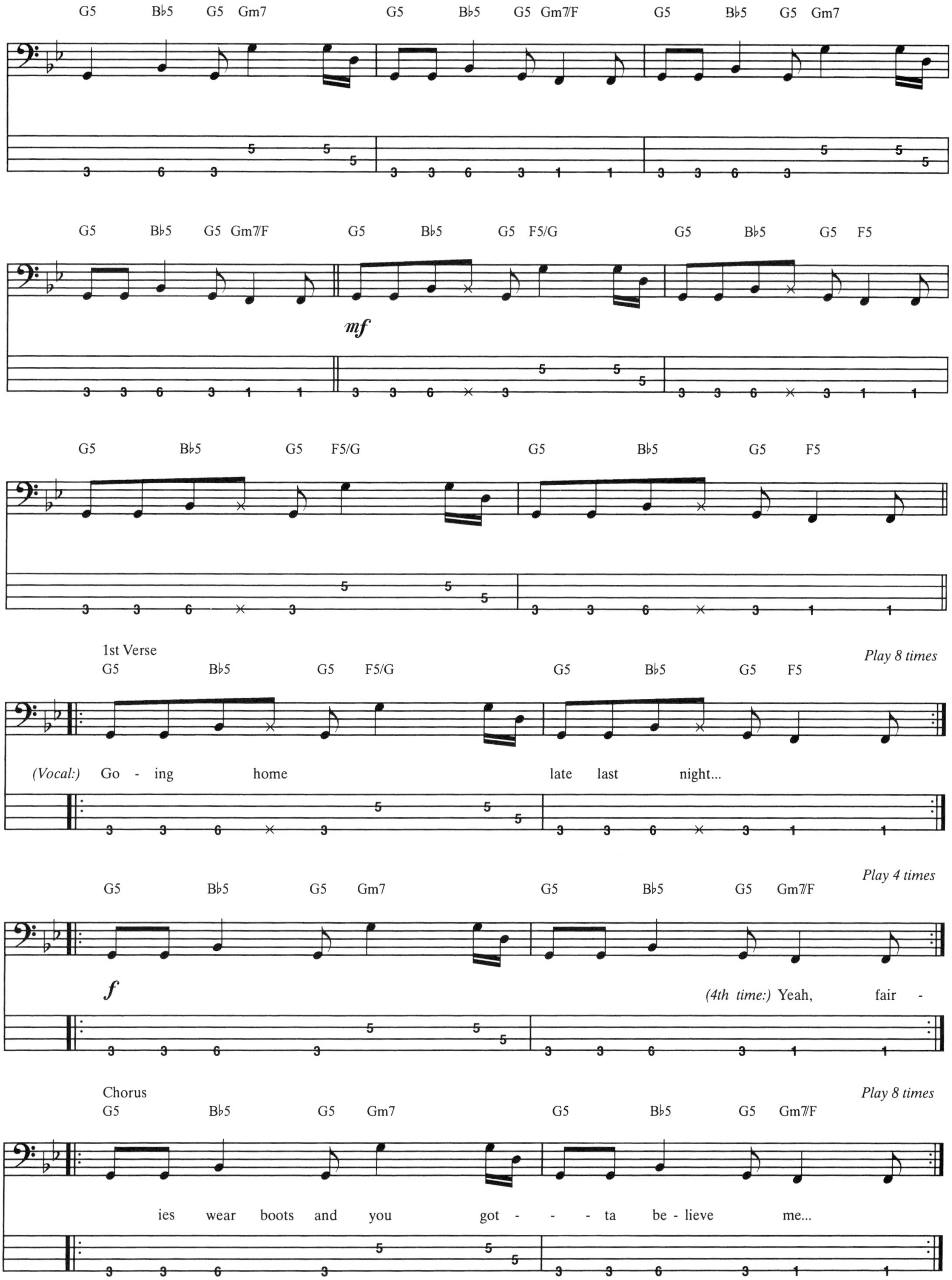

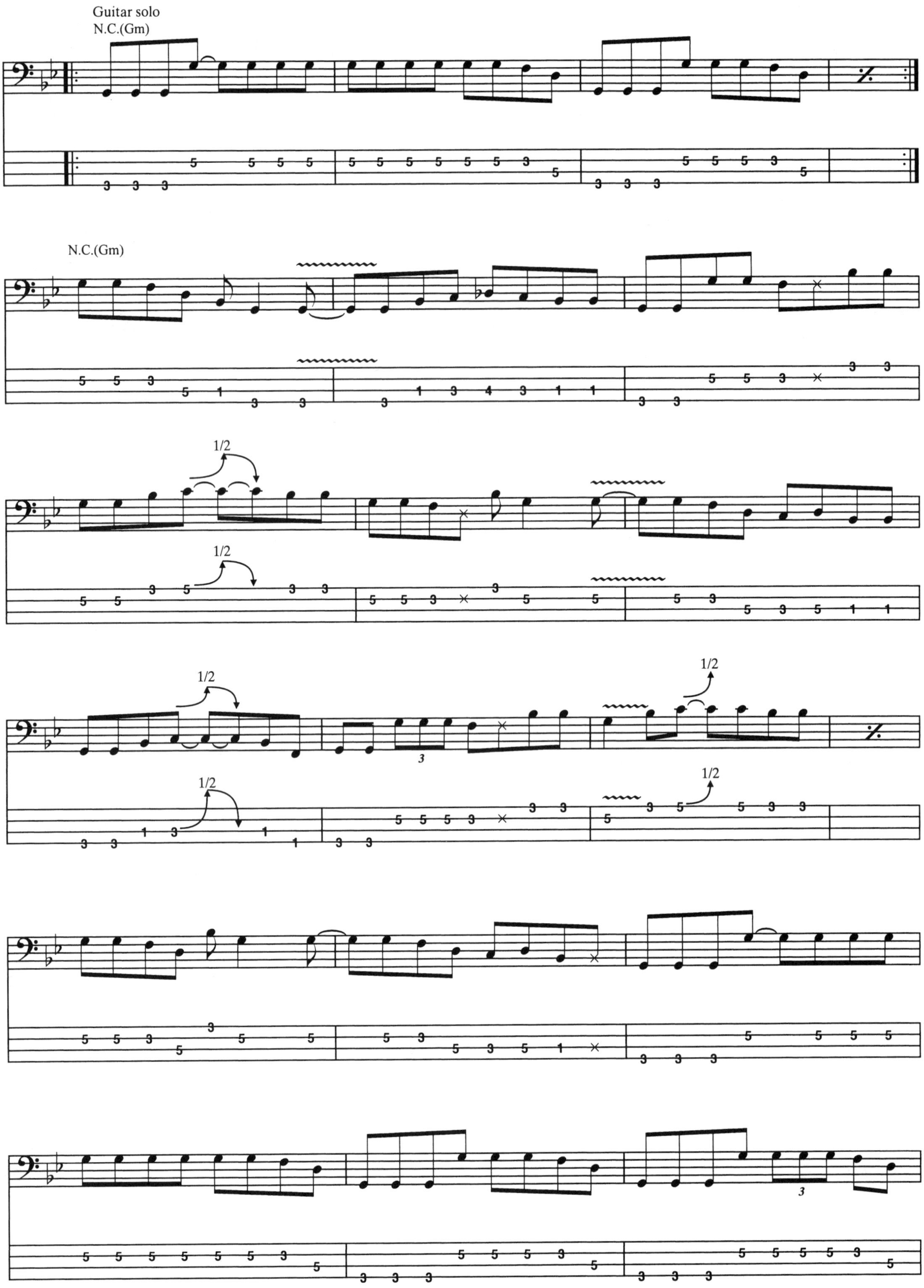
Guitar solo
N.C.(Gm)
N.C.(Gm)
1/2
1/2
1/2
1/2
1/2
1/2

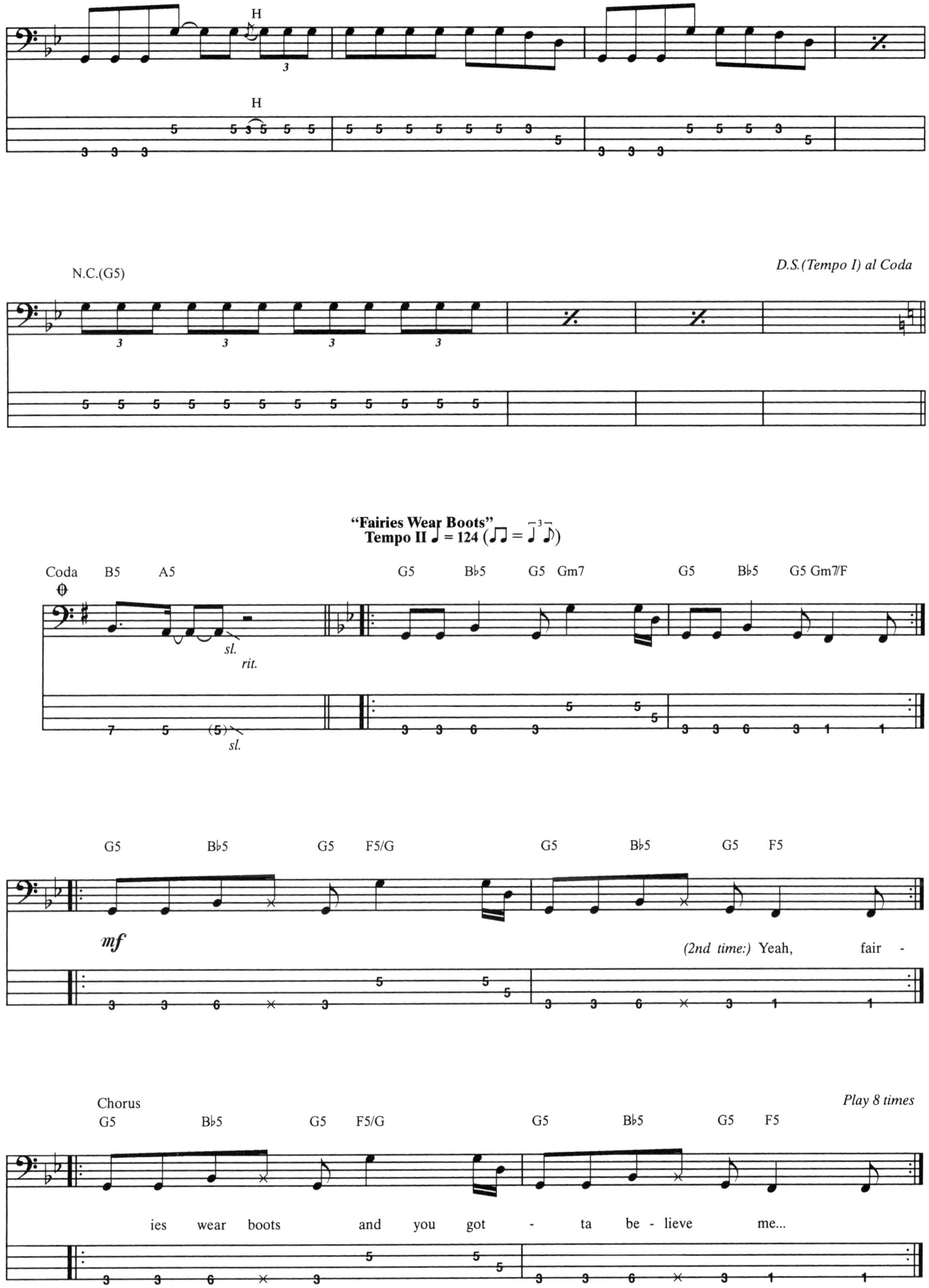
H
H
N.C.(G5)
D.S.(Tempo I) al Coda
"Fairies Wear Boots"
Tempo II ♩ = 124
Coda
B5
A5
sl.
rit.
sl.
G5 B♭5 G5 Gm7
G5 B♭5 G5 Gm7/F
G5 B♭5 G5 F5/G
G5 B♭5 G5 F5
mf
(2nd time:) Yeah, fair -
Chorus
G5 B♭5 G5 F5/G
G5 B♭5 G5 F5
Play 8 times
ies wear boots and you got - ta be - lieve me...

42

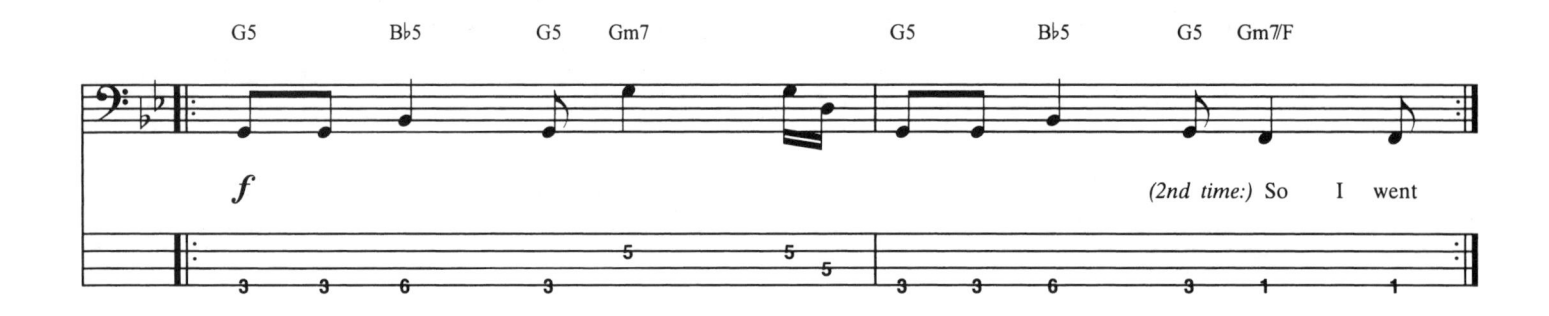

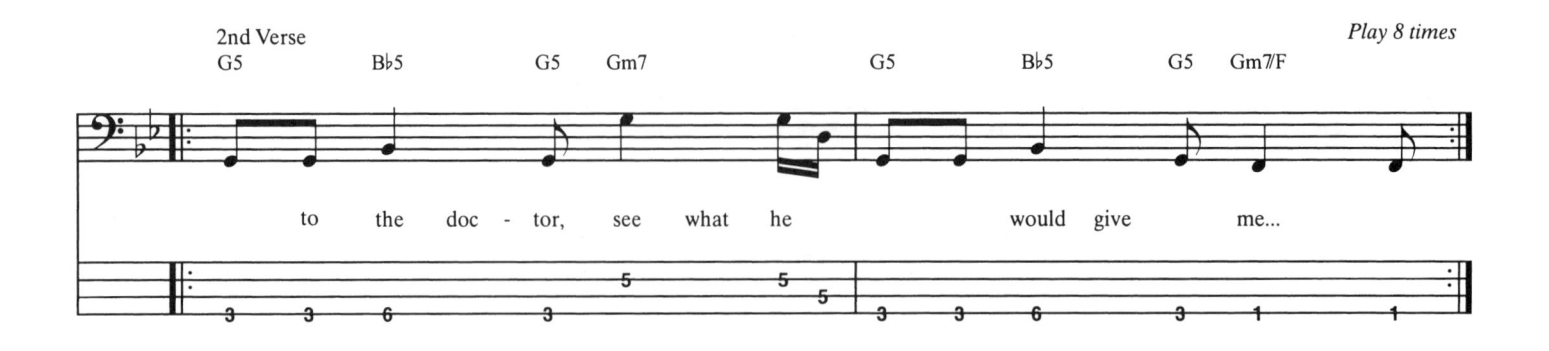

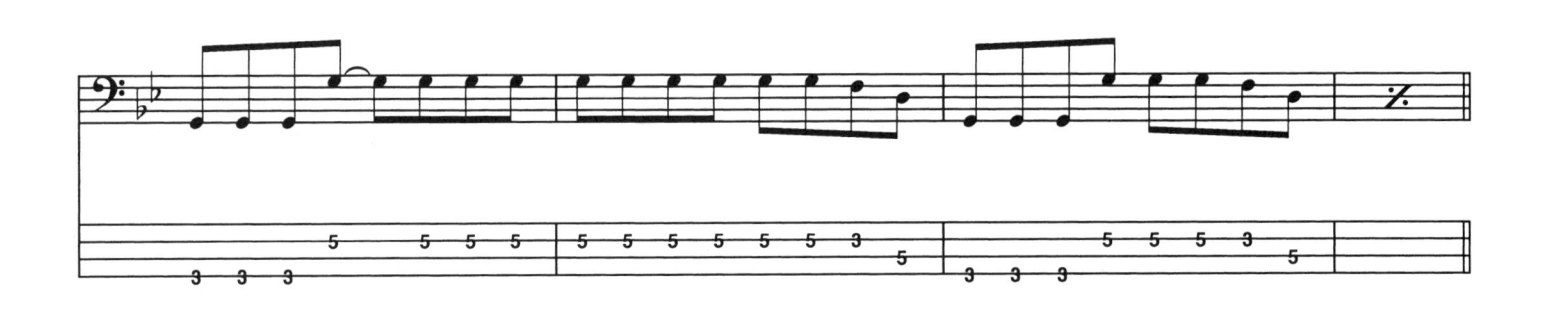

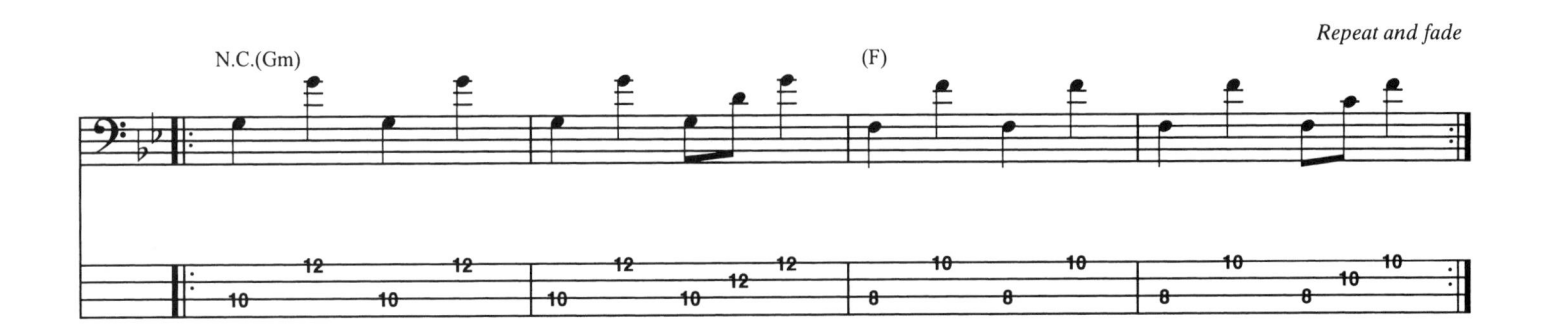

FEELS LIKE THE FIRST TIME

Words and Music by
Mick Jones

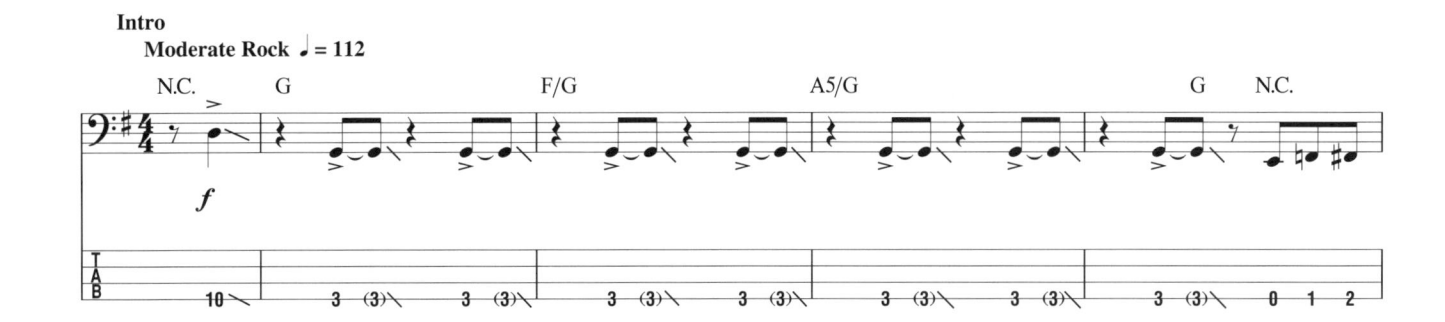

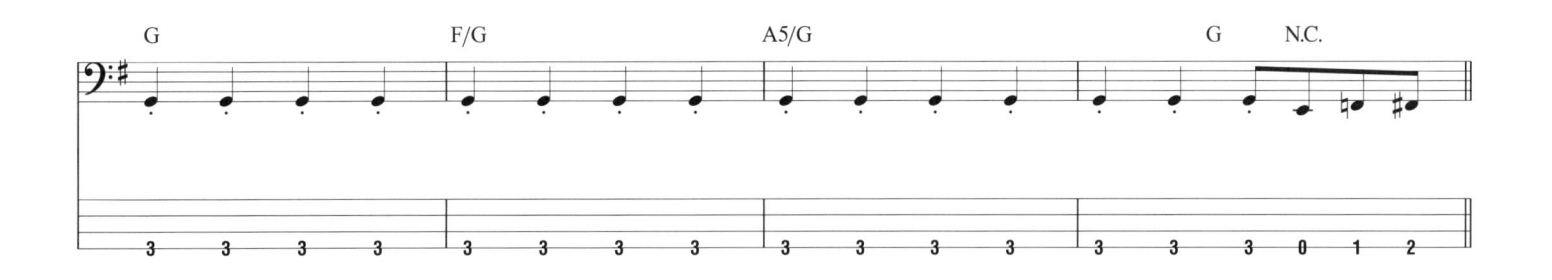

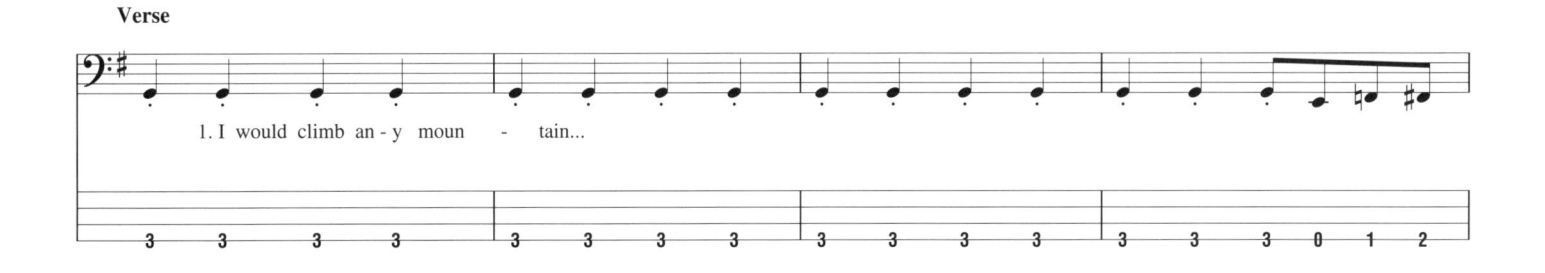

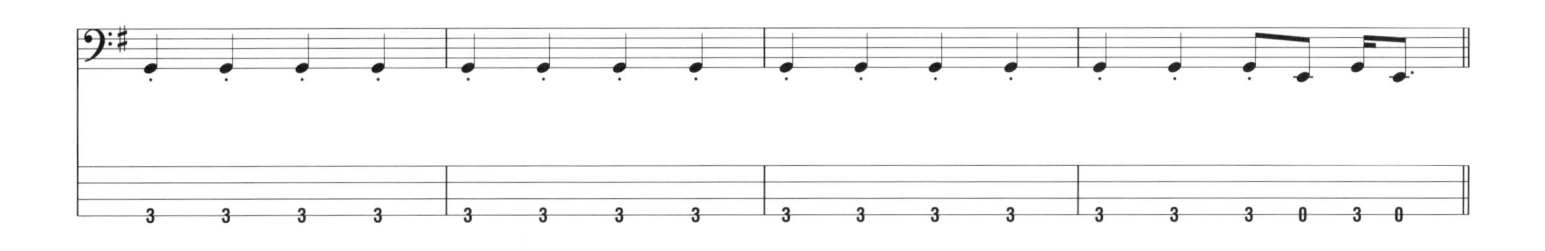

E/B
B
E/B
B
C
G5
Chorus
F/G
A5/G
G
N.C.
It feels like the first time...
G
F/G
A5/G
G
N.C.
Verse
G
F/G
Am/G
G
2. I have wait - ed a life - time...
F/G
Am/G
G
Pre-Chorus
D/A
A
D/A
A
And I know it must be the wom an in you

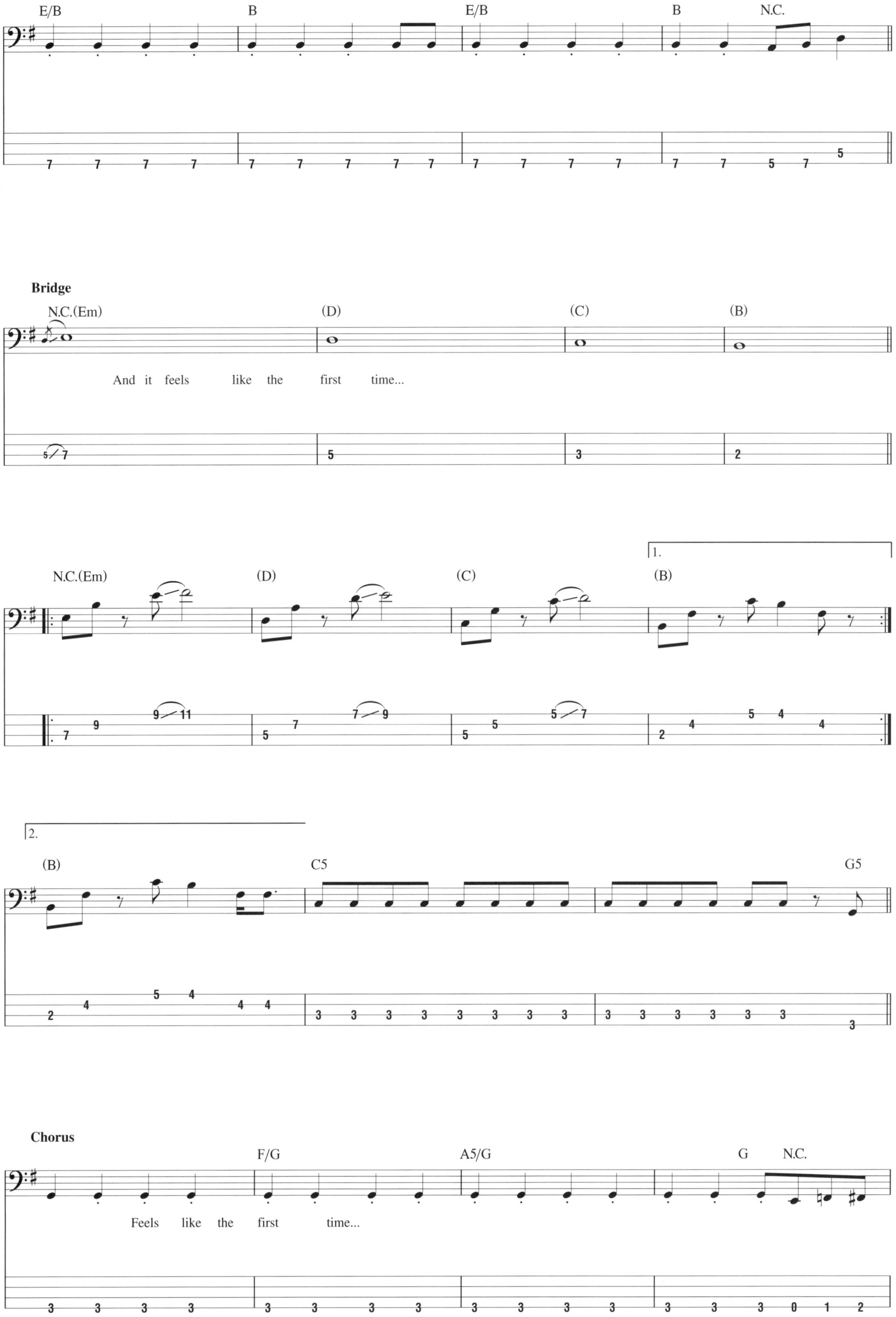
E/B
B
E/B
B
N.C.
Bridge
N.C.(Em)
(D)
(C)
(B)
And it feels like the first time...
1.
N.C.(Em)
(D)
(C)
(B)
2.
(B)
C5
G5
Chorus
F/G
A5/G
G
N.C.
Feels like the first time...

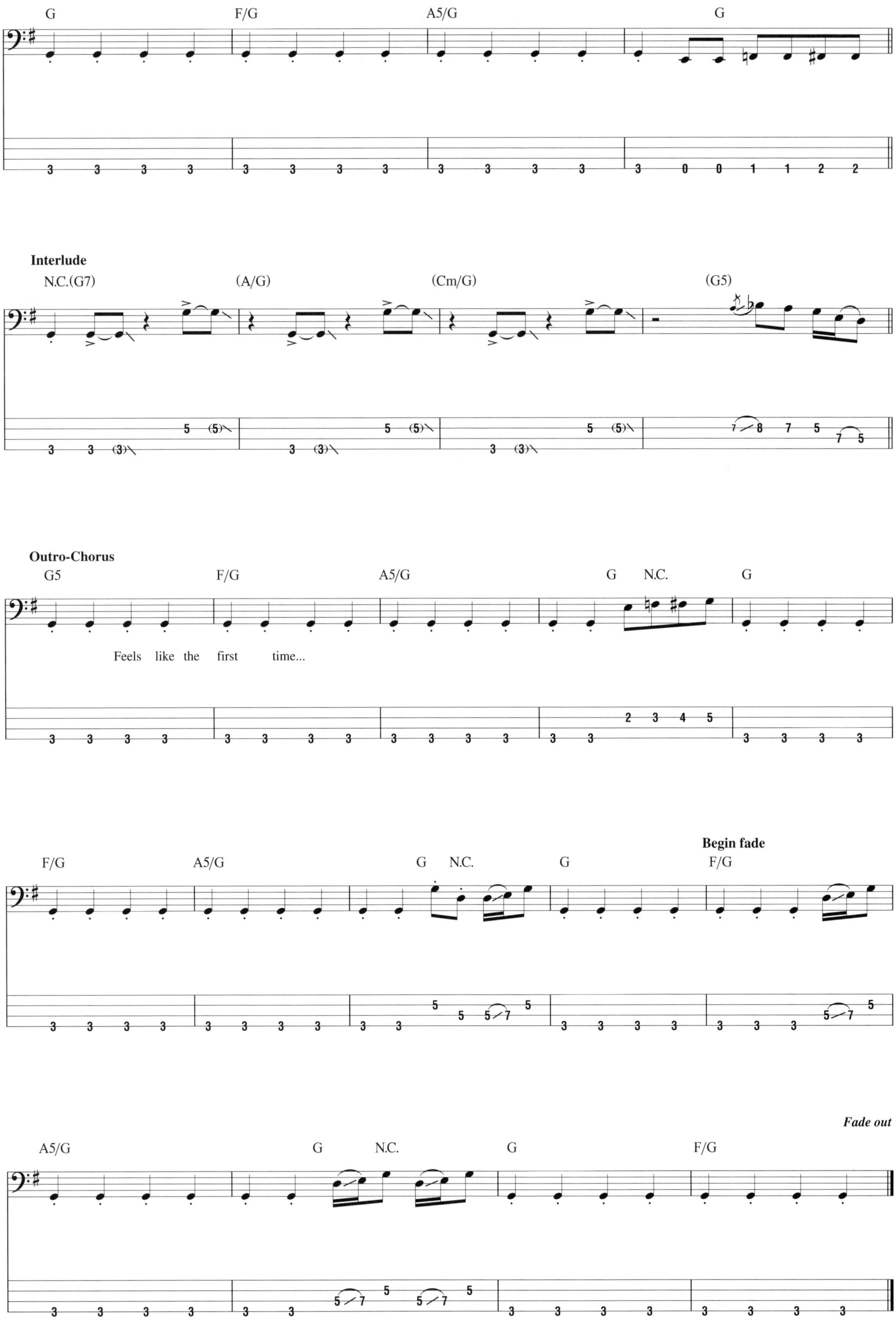

G F/G A5/G G
Interlude
N.C.(G7) (A/G) (Cm/G) (G5)
Outro-Chorus
G5 F/G A5/G G N.C. G
Feels like the first time...
F/G A5/G G N.C. G
Begin fade
F/G
Fade out
A5/G G N.C. G F/G

FM
from the film FM

Words and Music by
Walter Becker and Donald Fagen

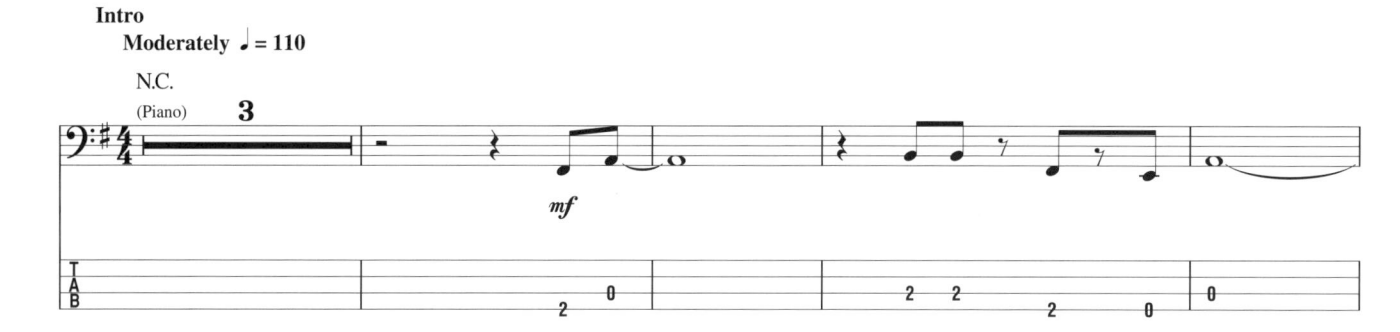

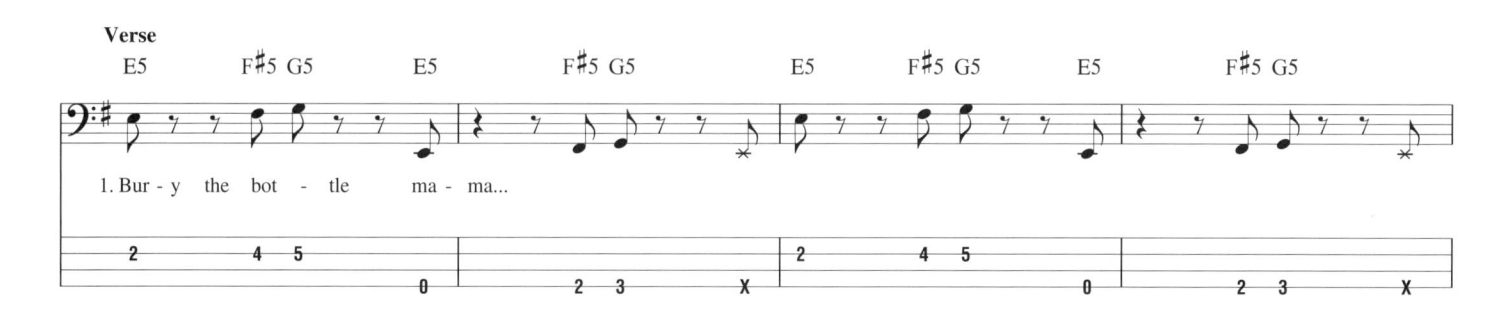

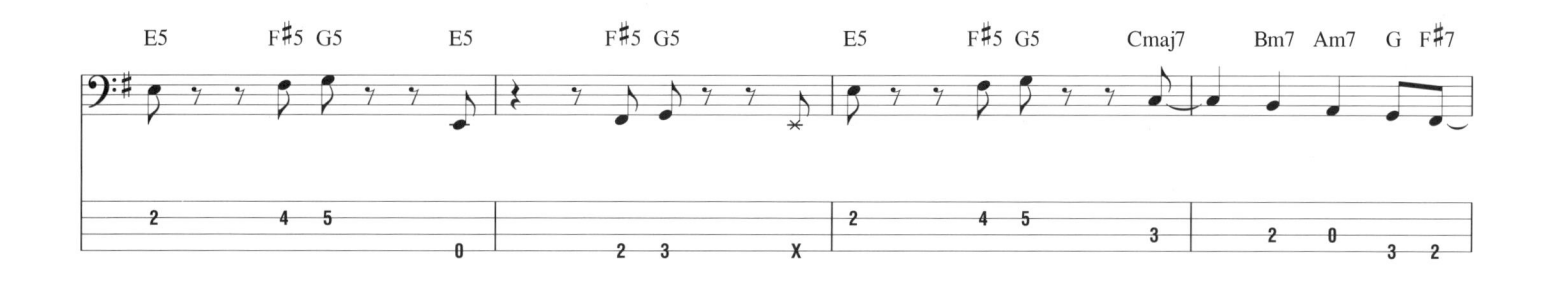

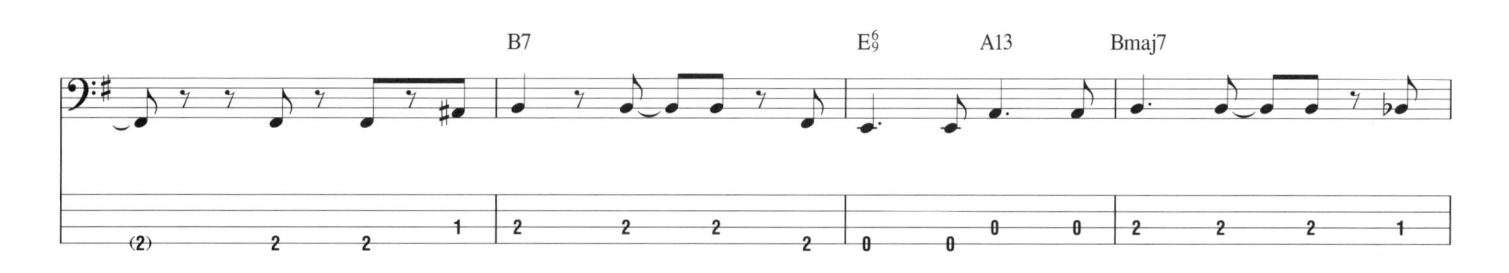

48

Saxophone Solo
Fmaj7
Em9
A13
Em9
C13
Dmaj7
C♯7♯9
Cmaj7
B7♯5
Em7
A7
Verse
C13
B7♯5
E5
F♯5 G5
E5
F♯5 G5
3. Give her some funked up Mu - zak...
E5
F♯5 G5
E5
F♯5 G5
E5
F♯5 G5
E5
F♯5 G5

E5 F♯5 G5 Cmaj7 Bm7 Am7 G F♯7 B7
Emaj13 G♯7♯5 C♯m11 F♯13 F♯m7
A7 D/E C7 B7♯5
Outro-Saxophone Solo
E5 F♯5 G5 E5 F♯5 G5
Play 5 times
E5 F♯5 G5 E5 F♯5 G5
E5 F♯5 G5 E5 F♯5 G5
Play 4 times
E5 F♯5 G5 E5 F♯5 G5

E5 F#5 G5 E5 F#5 G5 E5 F#5 G5 E5 F#5 G5
E5 F#5 G5 E5 F#5 G5 E5 F#5 G5 E5 F#5 G5
E5 F#5 G5 E5 F#5 G5 E5 F#5 G5 E5 F#5 G5
E5 F#5 G5 E5 F#5 G5 E5 F#5 G5 E5 F#5 G5
Repeat and fade
E5 F#5 G5 E5 F#5 G5 E5 F#5 G5 E5 F#5 G5

GETTING BETTER

Words and Music by
John Lennon and Paul McCartney

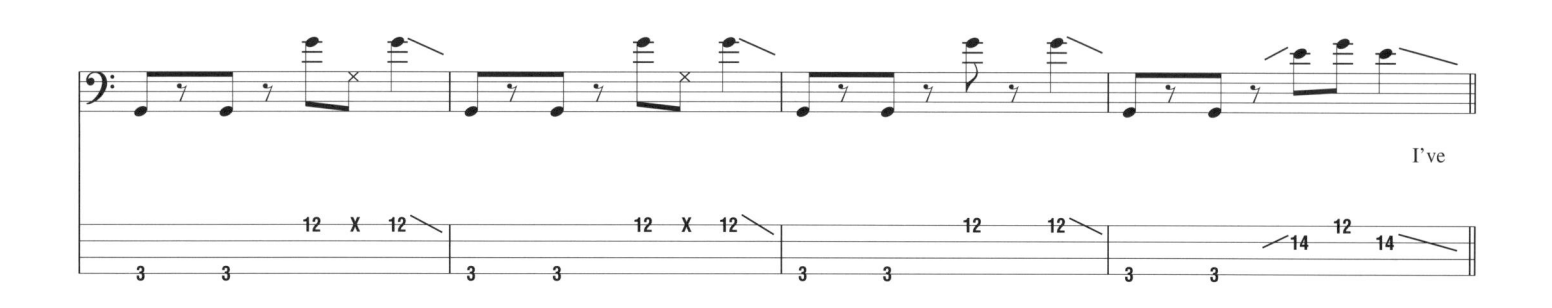

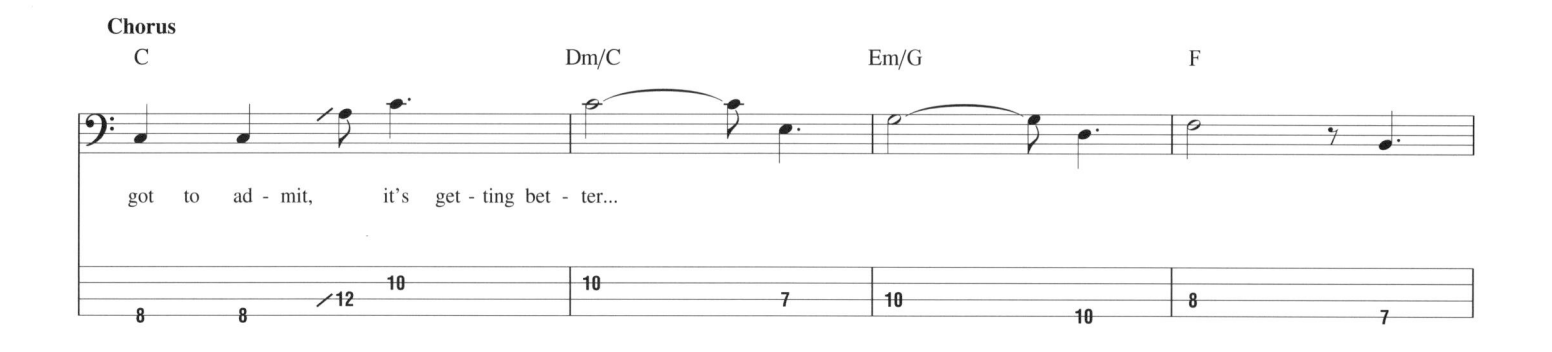

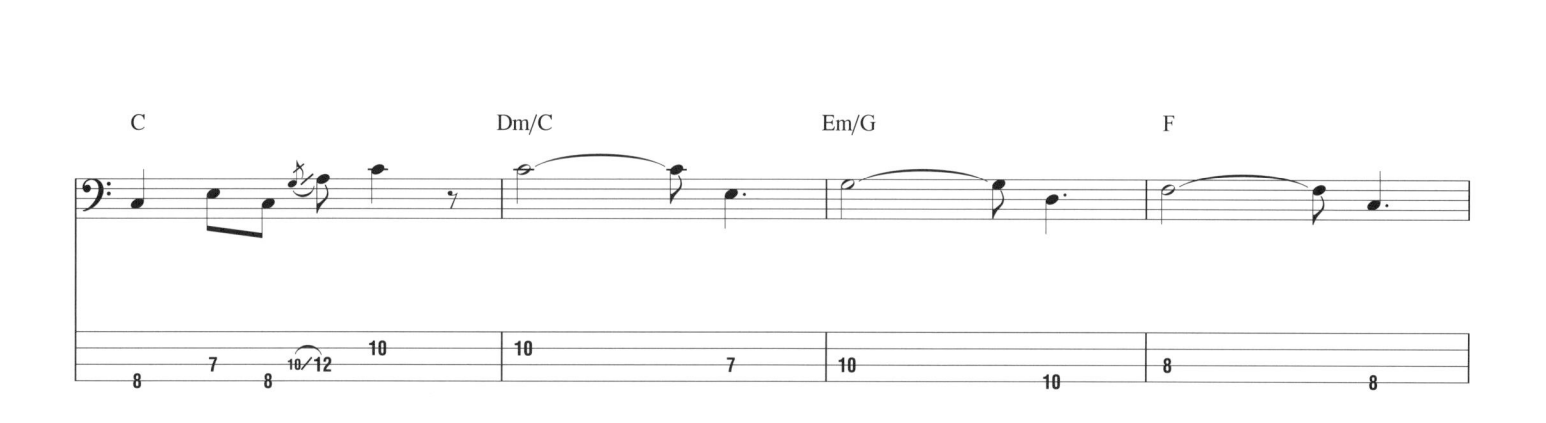

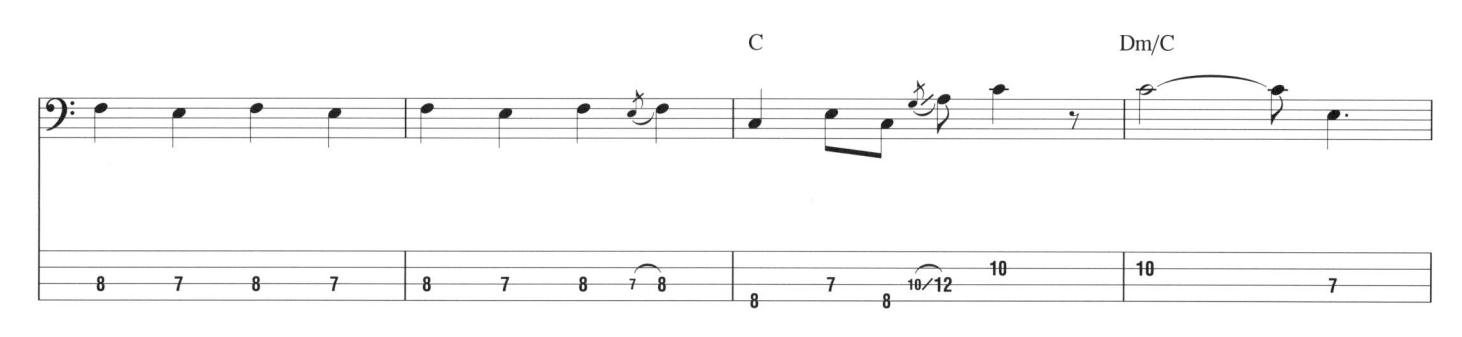

Verse

used to be an - gry young man...

I've

Chorus

got to ad - mit, it's get - ting bet - ter...

53

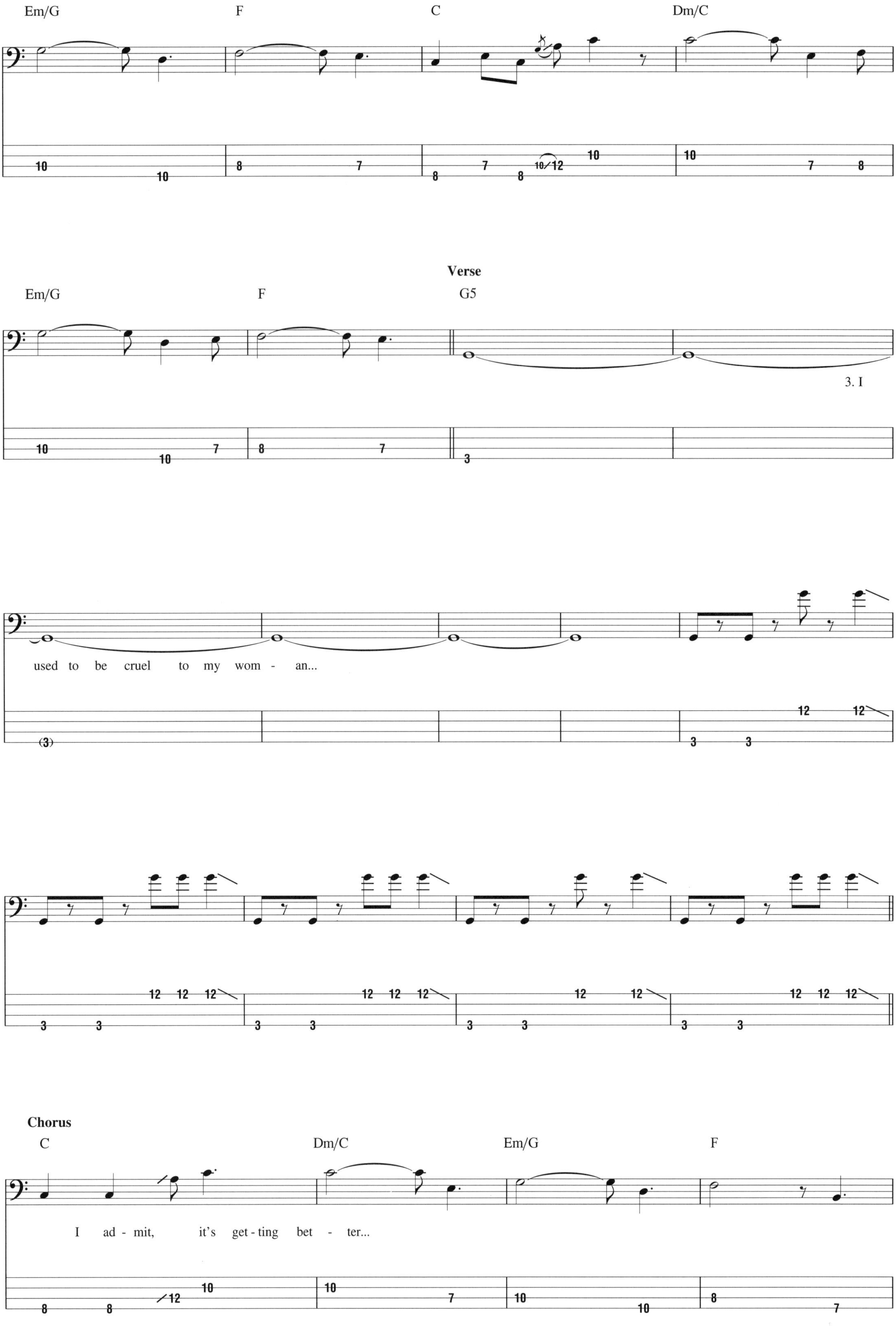
Em/G
F
C
Dm/C
Em/G
F
Verse
G5
3. I
used to be cruel to my wom - an...
Chorus
C
Dm/C
Em/G
F
I ad - mit, it's get - ting bet - ter...

C
Dm/C
Em/G
F
C
Dm/C
Em/G
F
C
Dm/C
Em/G
F
C
Begin fade
Fade out
(Guitar)
3
dim.

I WANT YOU BACK

Words and Music by
Freddie Perren, Alphonso Mizell,
Berry Gordy and Deke Richards

Moderate Soul ♩ = 100

Oh__ ba-by, give_ me one_ more chance....*(etc.)*

Chorus
Ab Eb/G Fm7 Eb Db Db/C Bbm7 Eb Fm7 Cm7 Db Ab
Bbm7 Eb Ab
Eb/G Fm7 Eb Db Db/C Bbm7 Eb Fm7 Cm7 Db Ab
Begin fade
Bbm7 Db/Eb Ab Eb/G Fm7 Eb
Db Db/C Bbm7 Eb Fm7 Cm7 Db Ab Bbm7 Db/Eb Ab
Eb/G Fm7 Eb
Fade out

LOWDOWN

Words and Music by
Boz Scaggs and David Paich

Intro
Moderately ♩ = 104

(Drums & guitar) — Em9 — A13 — *Play 4 times*

% Verse
Em9 — A13 — Em9

1. Ba - by's in - to run - nin' 'round...
2. Noth - in' you can't han - dle...
3. You ain't got to be so bad...

3rd time, w/ Bass Fill 1
A13 — Em9 — A13 — Em9

3rd time, w/ Bass Fill 1
A13 — Em9 — A13 — Em9

Chorus
A13 — Em9 — *2nd time, w/ Bass Fill 1* A13 — Em9

Who...

Copyright © 1976 by BMG Songs, Inc. and Hudmar Publishing
International Copyright Secured   All Rights Reserved

59

To Coda
A13
Bass Fill 1
End Bass Fill 1
Em9
A13
Em9
1.
A13
Em9
A13
Em9
2.
Bridge
A13
A13
Dmaj7
C#+
Am/C
B7
Em9
A13
Em9
A13
Em9

A13
Em9
A13
1., 2., 3.
4.
Guitar Solo
D.S. al Coda
F♯m7
B7
B7
Coda
Outro
A13
Dmaj7
C♯+
Am/C
B7
Em9
Repeat and fade
A13
Em9
A13

MESSAGE IN A BOTTLE

Music and Lyrics by
Sting

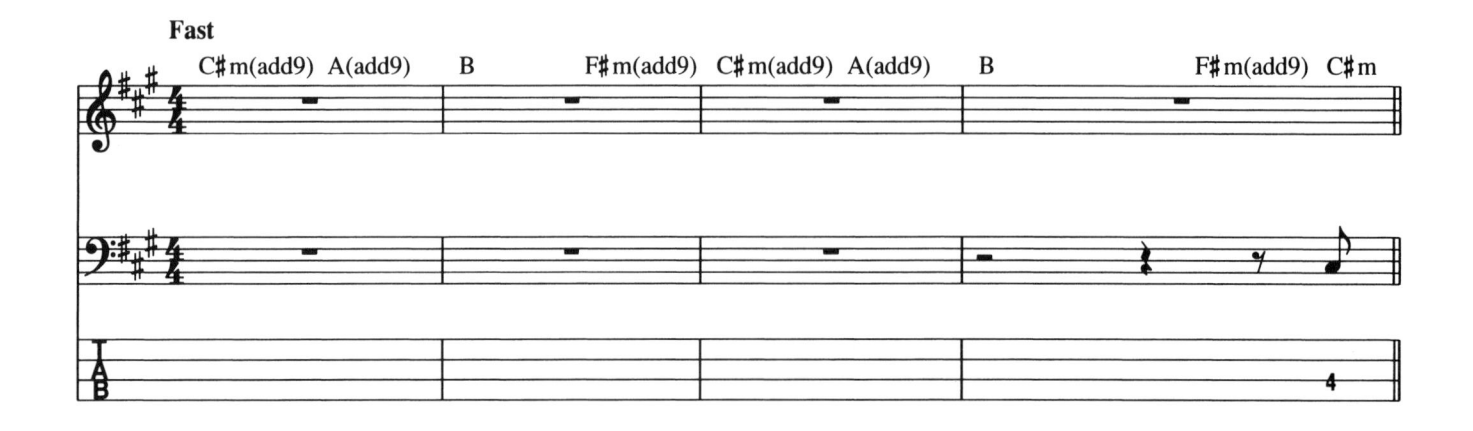

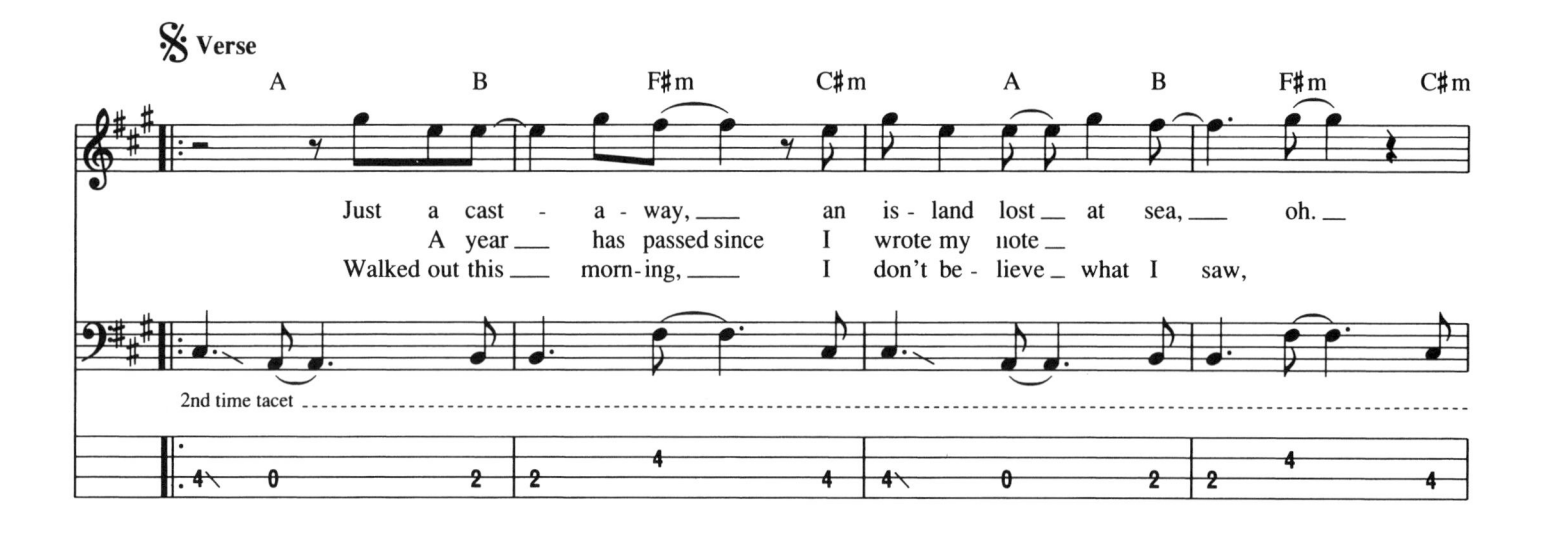

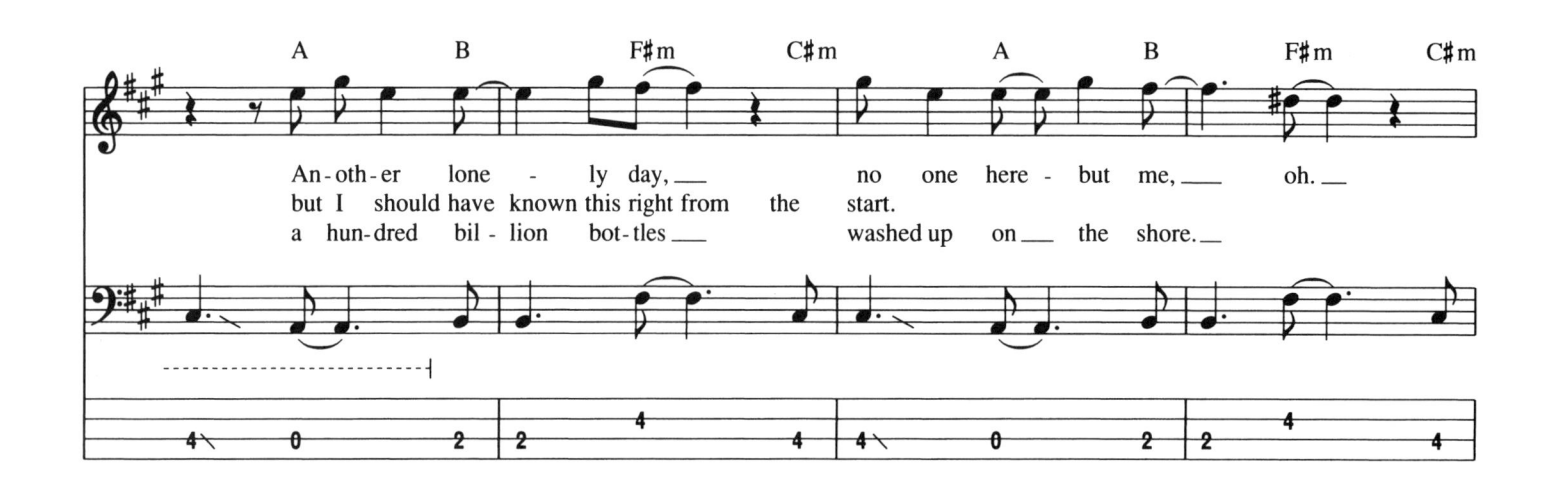

Just a cast-a-way, an is-land lost at sea, oh.
A year has passed since I wrote my note
Walked out this morn-ing, I don't be-lieve what I saw,

An-oth-er lone-ly day, no one here but me, oh.
but I should have known this right from the start.
a hun-dred bil-lion bot-tles washed up on the shore.

© 1979 G.M. SUMNER
Administered by EMI MUSIC PUBLISHING LIMITED
All Rights Reserved   International Copyright Secured   Used by Permission

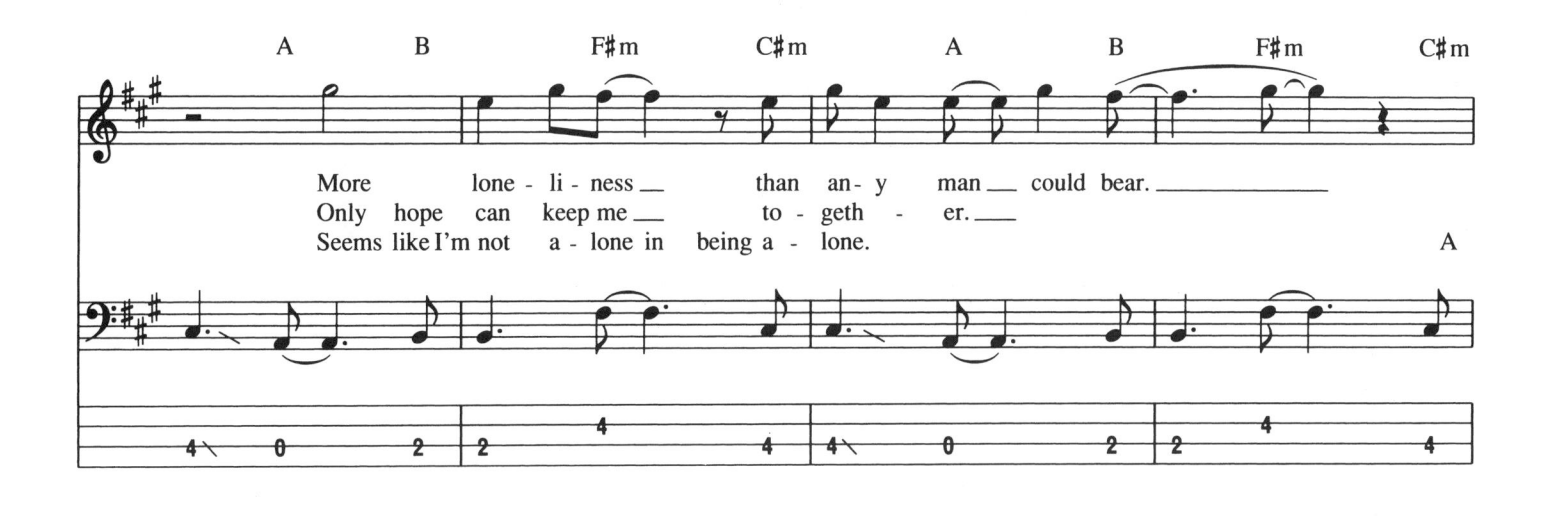

More lone-li-ness ___ than an-y man ___ could bear. ___
Only hope can keep me ___ to-geth-er. ___
Seems like I'm not a-lone in being a-lone.

Res-cue me ___ be-fore ___ I fall ___ in-to ___ des-pair, ___ oh. ___
Love ___ can mend ___ your life ___ but love ___ can break ___ your heart. ___
hun-dred bil-lion cast-a-ways ___ look-ing for ___ a home.

Chorus

I'll send ___ an S. ___ O. ___ S. ___ to the world. ___ I'll send ___ and S. ___ O. ___ S. ___ to the world. ___

___ I hope _ that some-one gets _ my, I hope _ that some-one gets _ my,

64

D.S. al Coda

Coda

mes- sage in a bot - tle,

mes- sage in a bot - tle,

mes- sage in a bot - tle, oh yeah.

Repeat and Fade

send- ing out an S. O. S. I'm

2nd time

MINUTE BY MINUTE

Words by Michael McDonald and Lester Abrams
Music by Michael McDonald

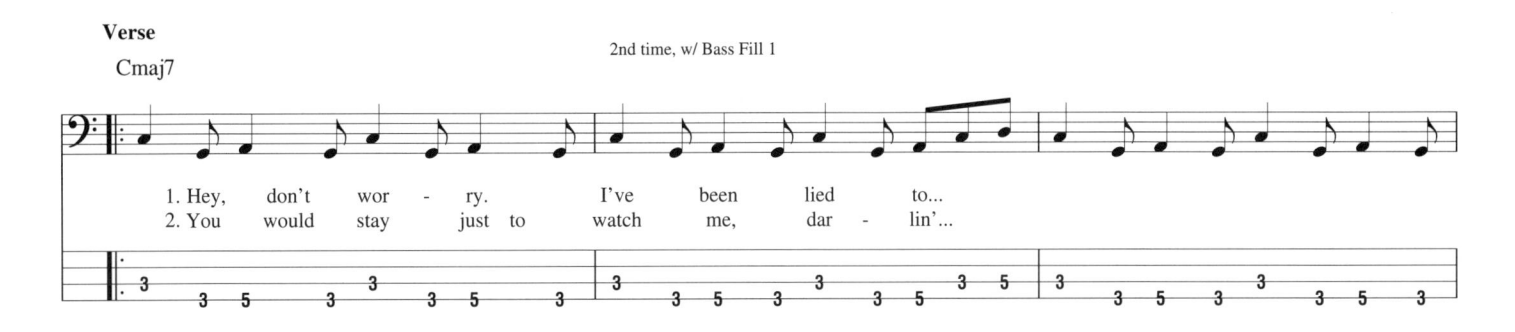

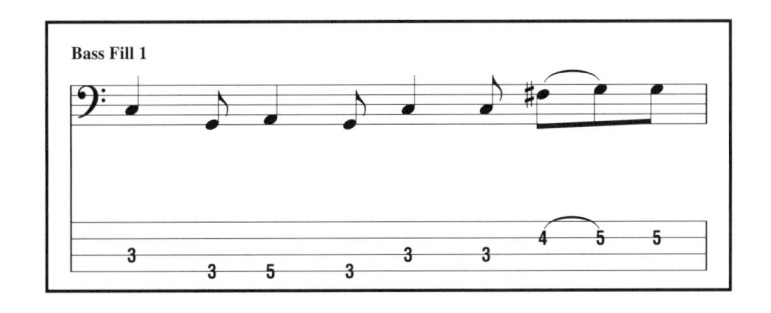

Verse

Cmaj7 — 2nd time, w/ Bass Fill 1

1. Hey, don't wor - ry. I've been lied to...
2. You would stay just to watch me, dar - lin'...

F13sus4   F13

Am7/G   F/G   F13sus4

F13   Am7/G   F/G

Bass Fill 1

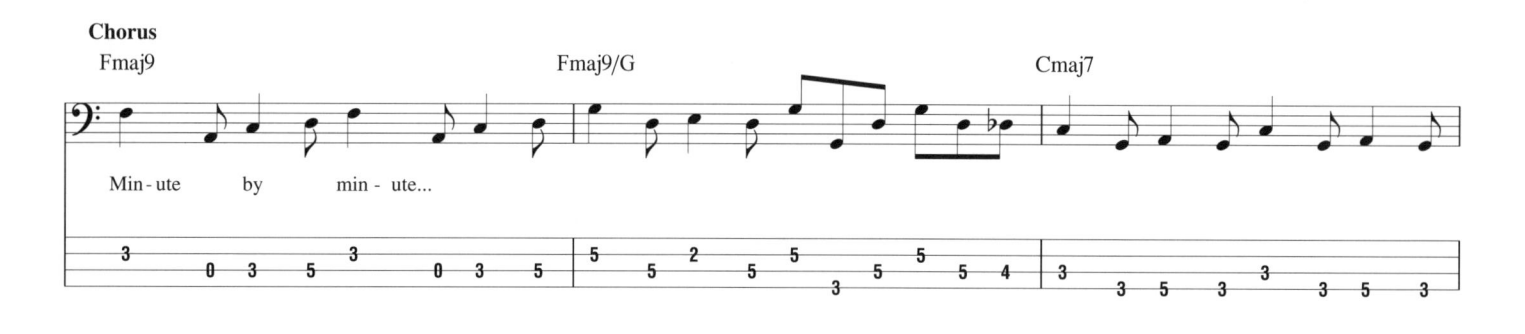

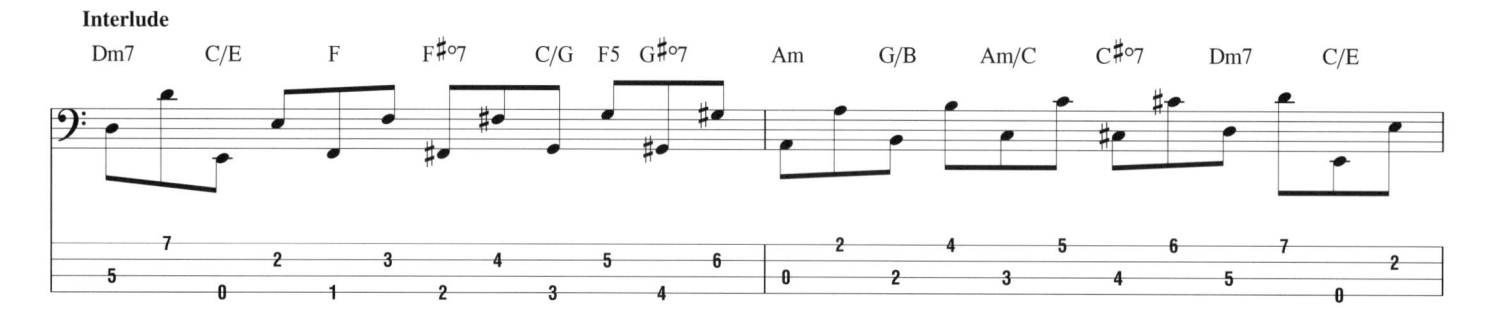

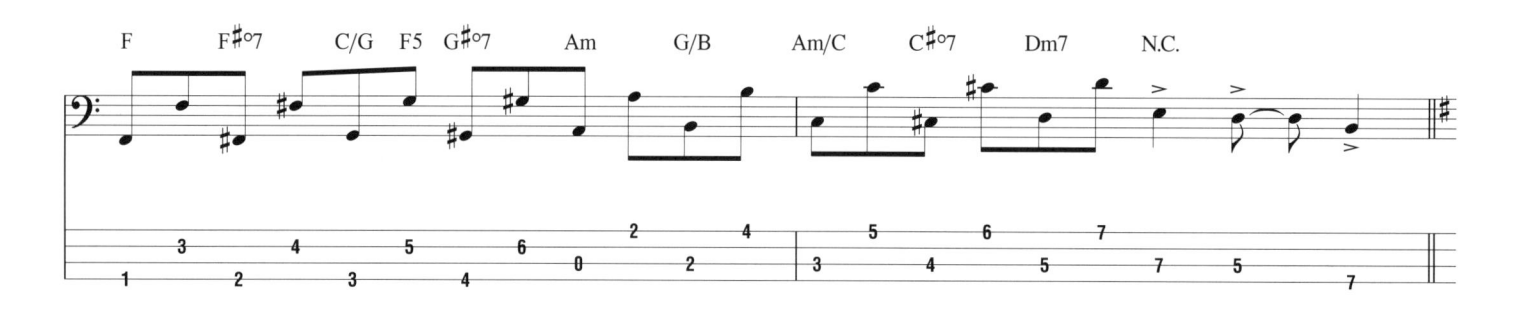

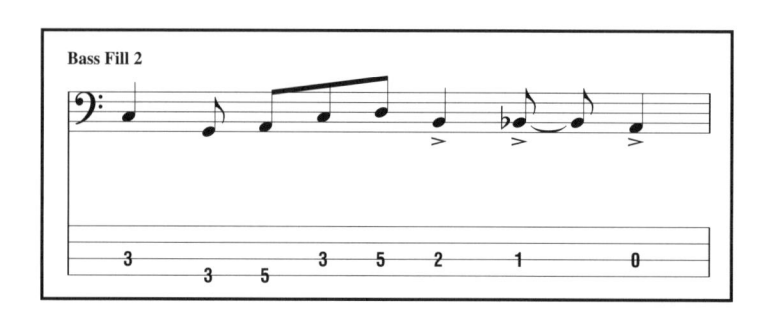

Chorus

Min-ute by min-ute...

Bridge
Em7
Cmaj9
Call my name and I'll be gone...
Am7sus4
Am7
Am7sus4
Am7
Cmaj7/D
C/D
Cmaj7/D
C/D
Cmaj7/D
Chorus
Cmaj9
Cmaj9/D
Min-ute by min-ute...
Gmaj7
F♯m7 F7 Em7 Cmaj9
Repeat and fade
Cmaj9/D
Gmaj7
F♯m7 F7 Em7

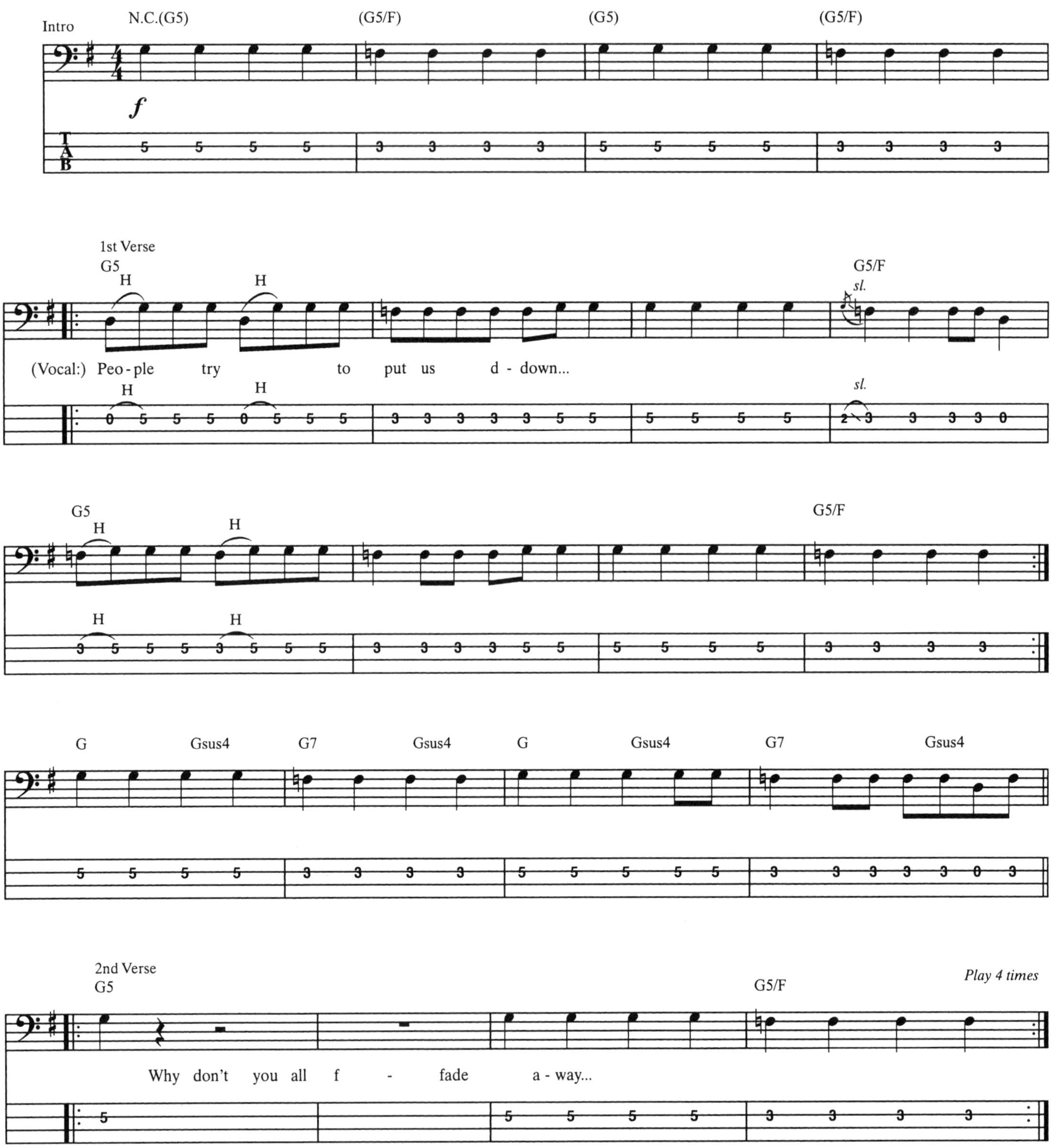

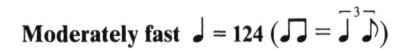

G Gsus4 G7 Gsus4 G Gsus4 G7 Gsus4
Guitar/Bass solo
G5 G6 G7 G6
1/4
G5 G6 G7 G6
1/4
sl.
G5 G6 G7 G6
full
sl.
G5 G6 G7 G6
G Gsus4 G7 Gsus4 G Gsus4 G7 Gsus4
3rd Verse
A5 A5/G
Play 4 times
Why don't you all f - fade a - way...

72

Talk - in' 'bout my gen - er - a - tion...

Play 4 times

ROCK & ROLL - PART II
(The Hey Song)

Words and Music by
Mike Leander and Gary Glitter

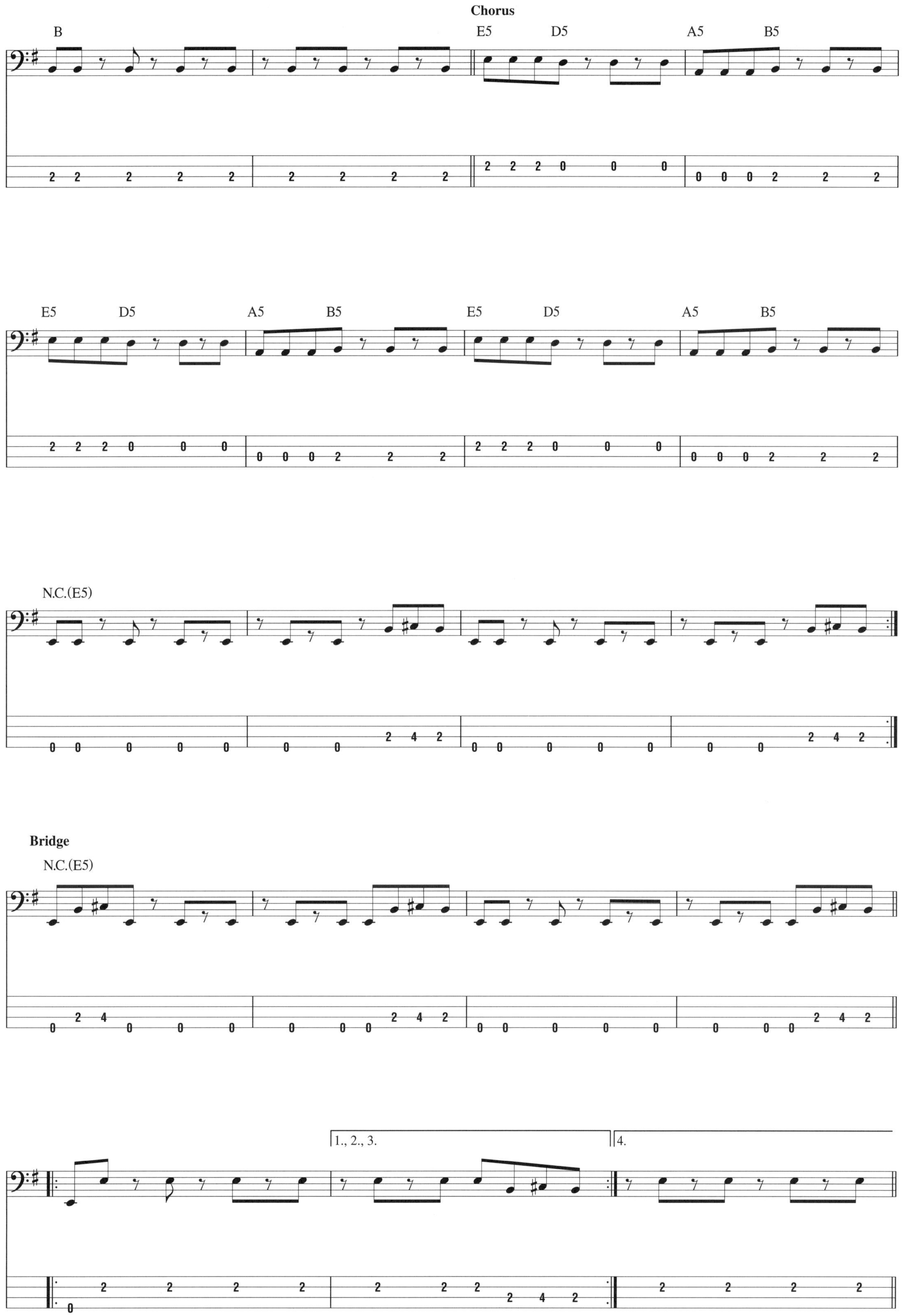
Chorus
B
E5 D5 A5 B5
E5 D5 A5 B5 E5 D5 A5 B5
N.C.(E5)
Bridge
N.C.(E5)
1., 2., 3.
4.

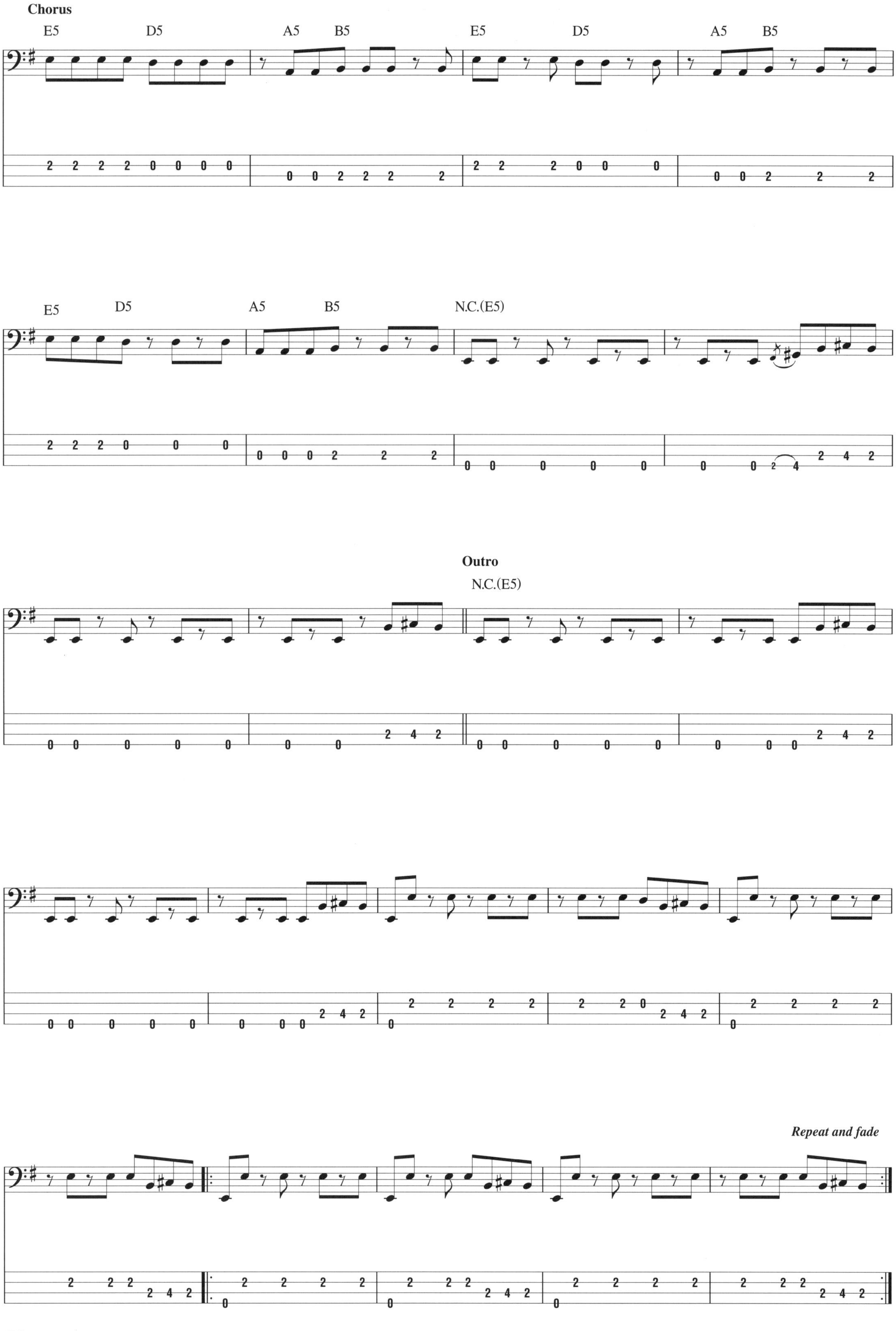
Chorus
E5 D5 A5 B5 E5 D5 A5 B5
E5 D5 A5 B5 N.C.(E5)
Outro
N.C.(E5)
Repeat and fade

ROSANNA

Words and Music by
David Paich

E♭sus2
Dm7
Pre-Chorus
Double-time feel
Gm
F/A B♭
E♭/B♭
mf
Not quite a year since she went a - way...
B♭ F
Gm
F/A B♭
End double-time feel
F5 E♭
f
B♭ F
Chorus
B♭ B♭/C Cm7
E♭sus2
Meet you all the way...
*T T T T T
*Strike ("slap") string w/ R.H. thumb.
B♭ F B♭/G B♭/C Cm7 E♭sus2
T T T T T
B♭ F B♭/G B♭/C Cm7 E♭sus2
T T T T T

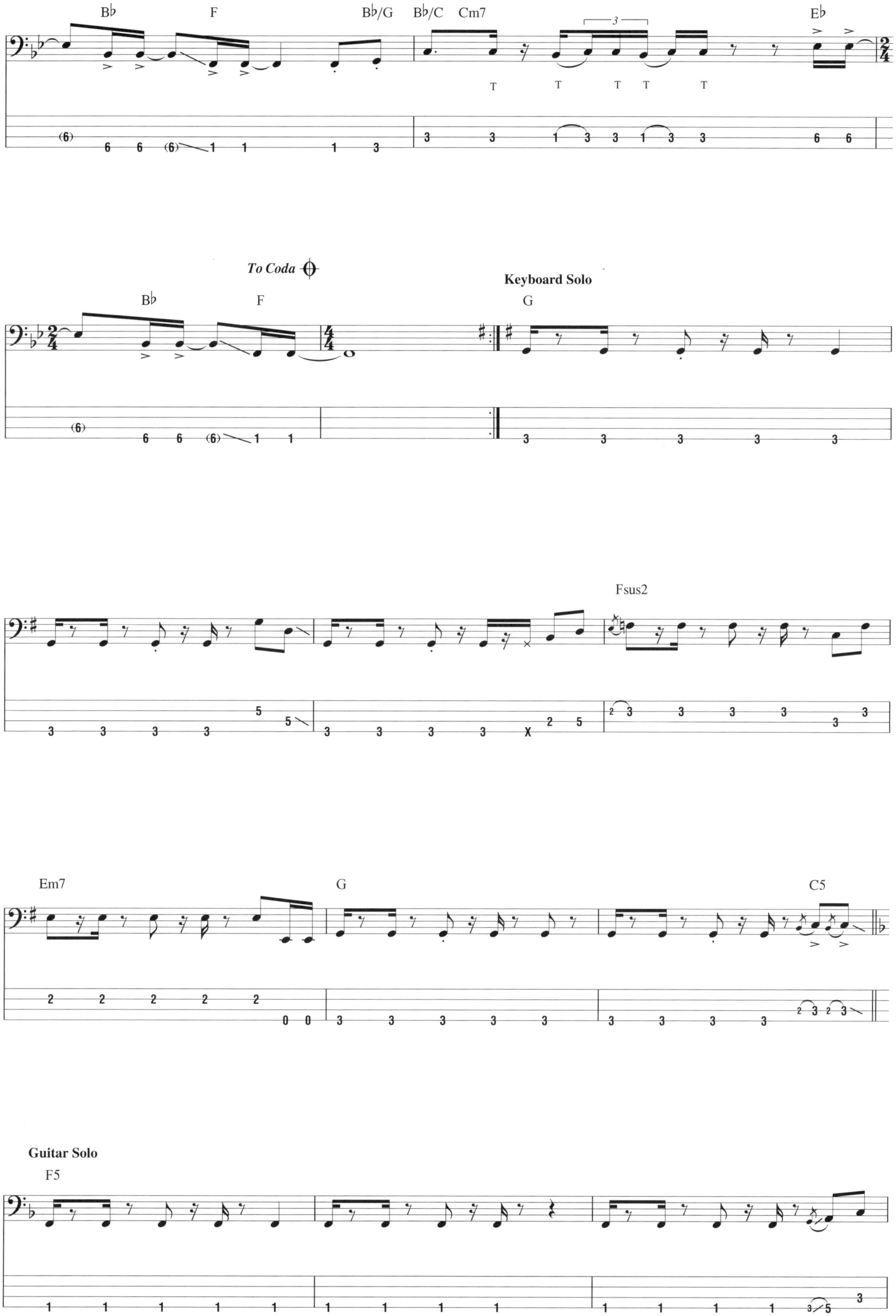
B♭
F
B♭/G
B♭/C
Cm7
E♭
To Coda
B♭
F
Keyboard Solo
G
Fsus2
Em7
G
C5
Guitar Solo
F5

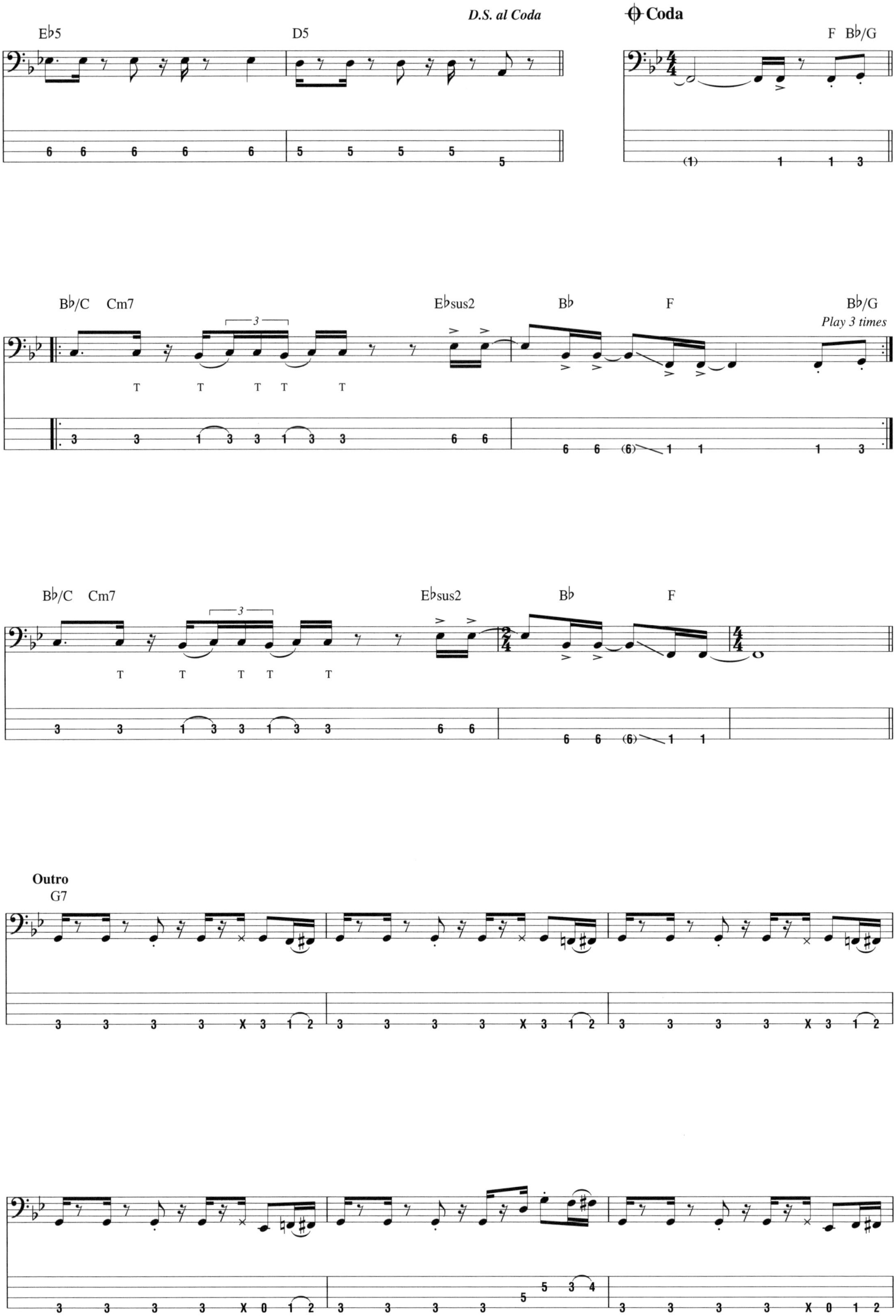
D.S. al Coda
Coda
E♭5
D5
F B♭/G
B♭/C Cm7
E♭sus2
B♭
F
B♭/G
Play 3 times
B♭/C Cm7
E♭sus2
B♭
F
Outro
G7

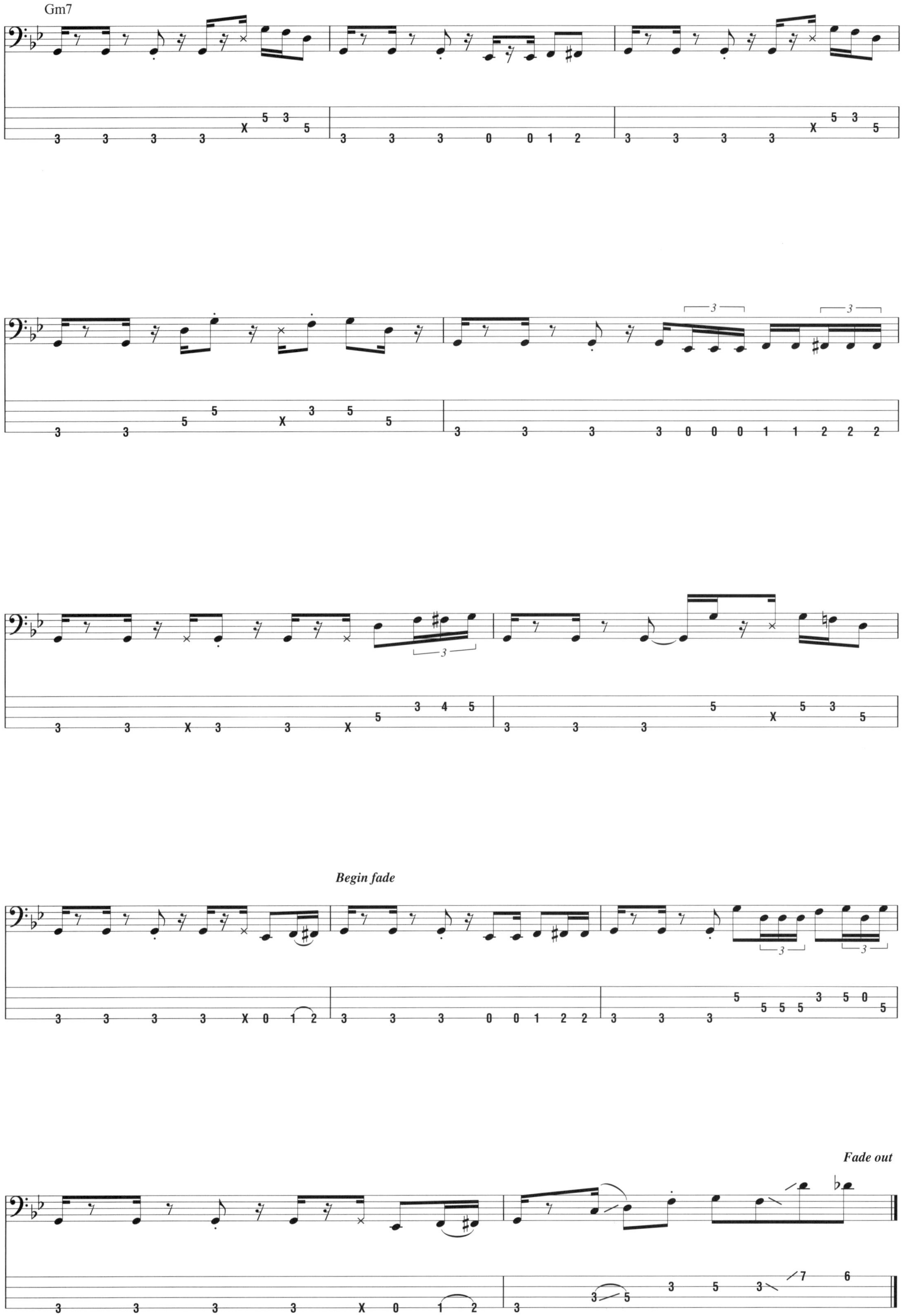
Gm7
Begin fade
Fade out

ROUNDABOUT

Words and Music by
Jon Anderson and Steve Howe

2.3.
F add9
G C F C
2
poco rit.
a tempo
3
G C F C F C G
f
C F C B♭
G C F C F C G
C F C B♭
Am Bm C D Em7
H H H H
H H
H H

N.C.
3rd, 4th Verses
Em7
Am7
Bm
Bm/A
Gmaj7
poco rit.
F add9
To Coda
G C F C F C G
a tempo
C F C B♭
G C F C F C G

C F C Bb G C F C F C G
C F C Bb G C F C F C G
C F C Bb Am Bm C D Em7
N.C.
Riff A (Bass I)
N.C. (Em)
Play 10 times
w/Riff A (Bass I)
Bass II
*Last time only
sl.
H

2.
Bass I
Bass II
Free time
Interlude
Bb G F Bb Eb
Organ solo
G C F C F G5 G
C F C Bb G C F C F G5 G

87

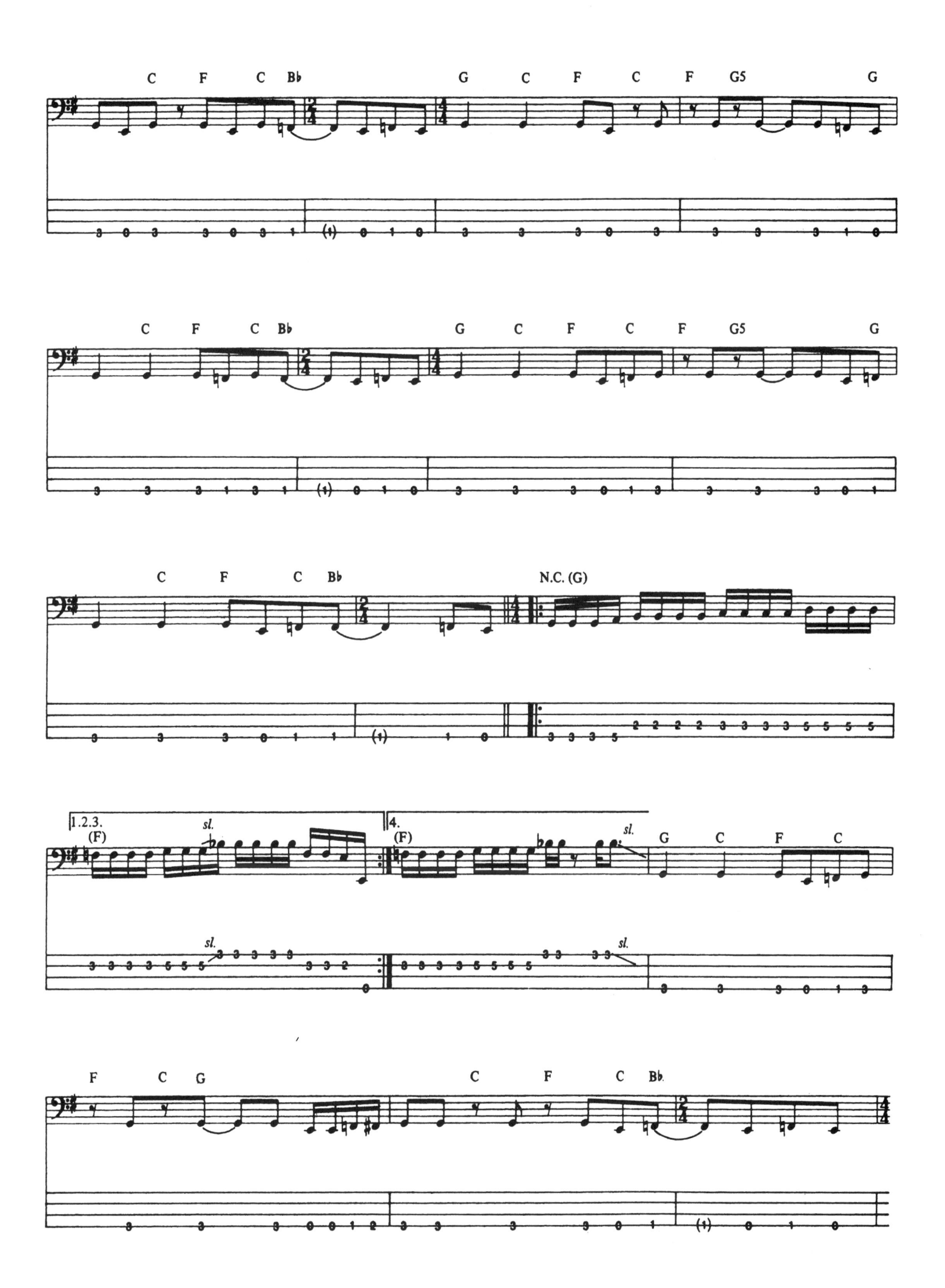

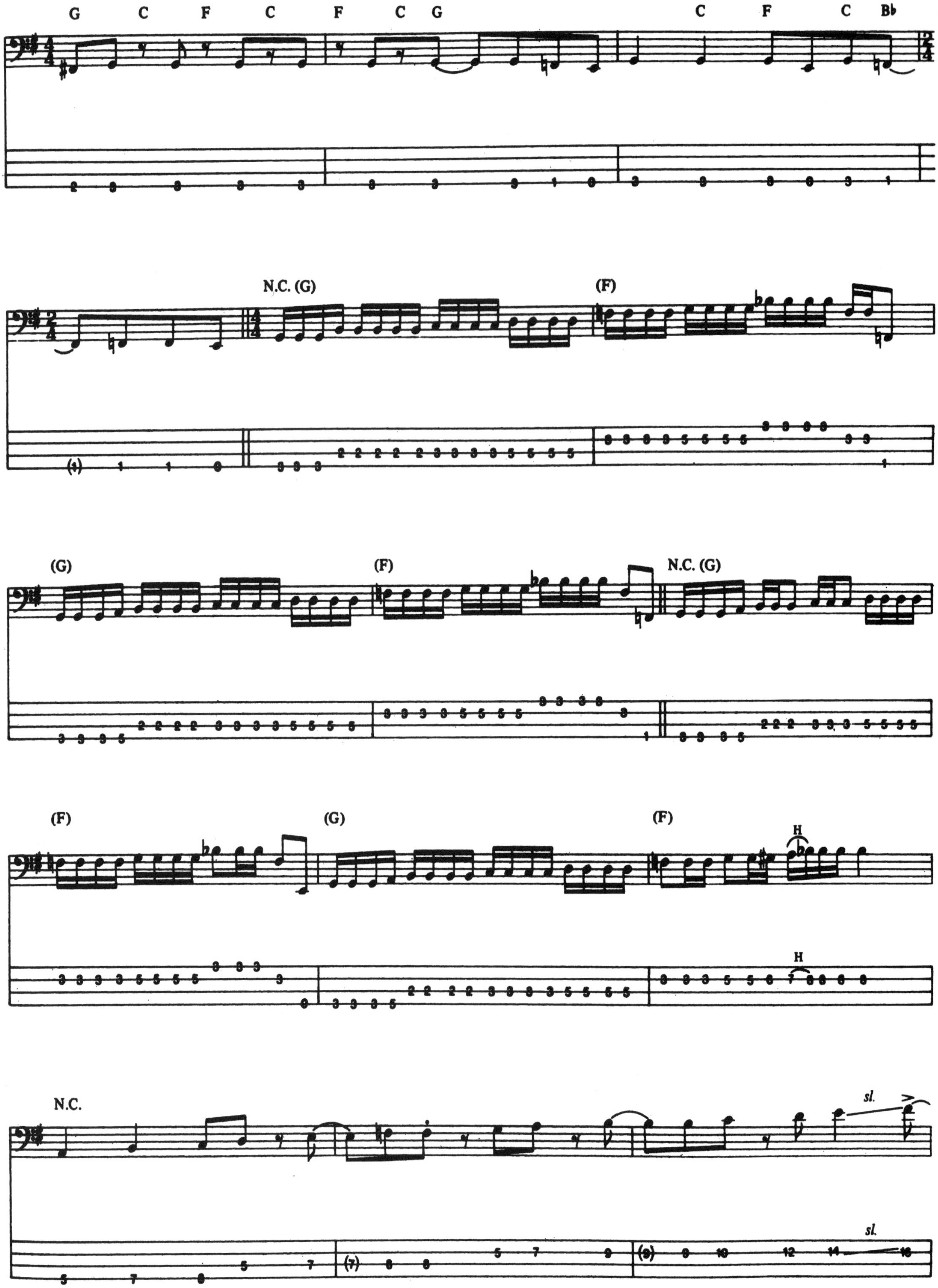
G C F C F C G C F C Bb
N.C. (G)
(F)
(G)
(F)
N.C. (G)
(F)
(G)
(F)
H
N.C.
sl.

89

SATCH BOOGIE

By Joe Satriani

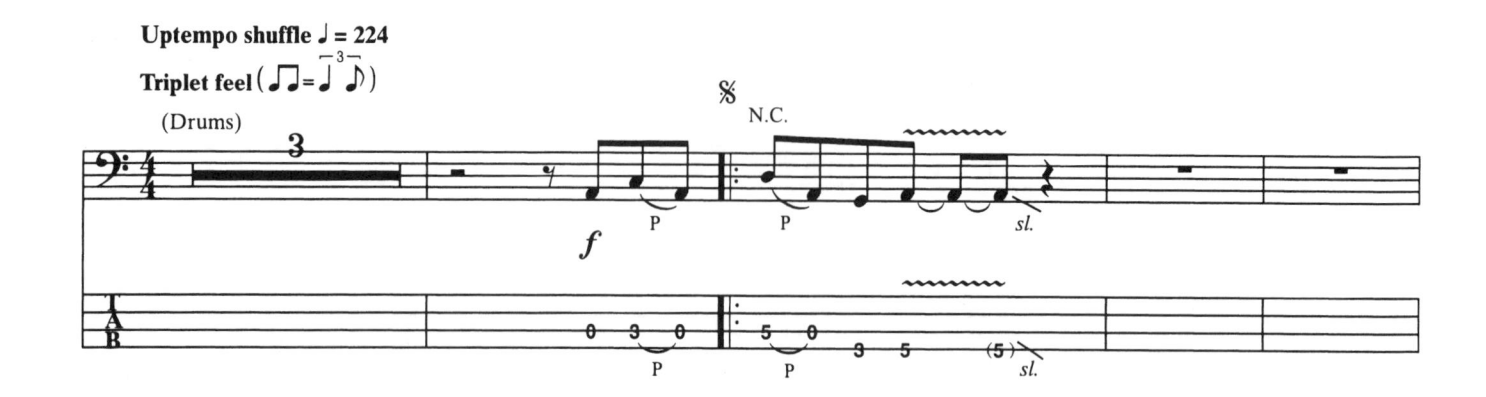

91

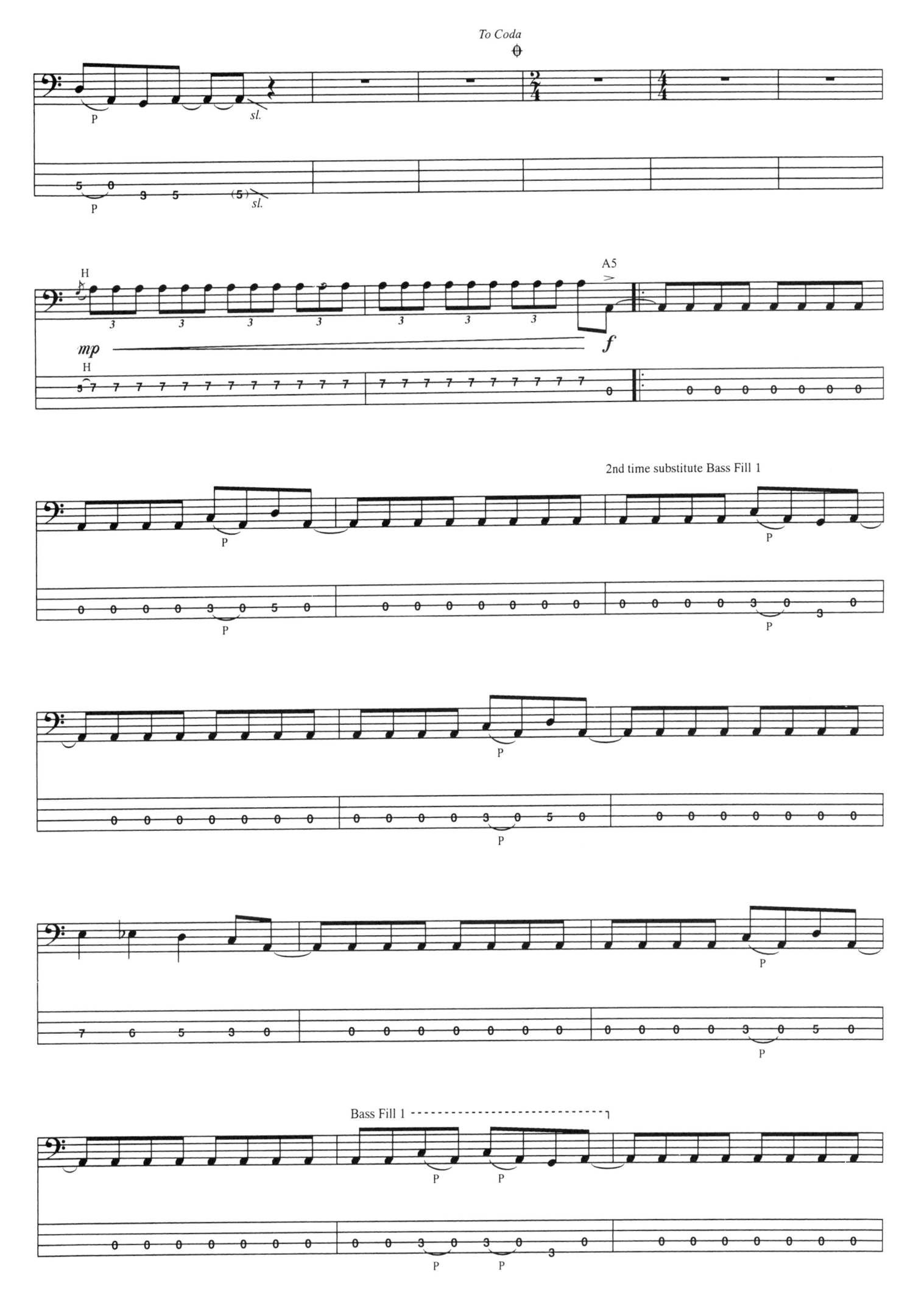

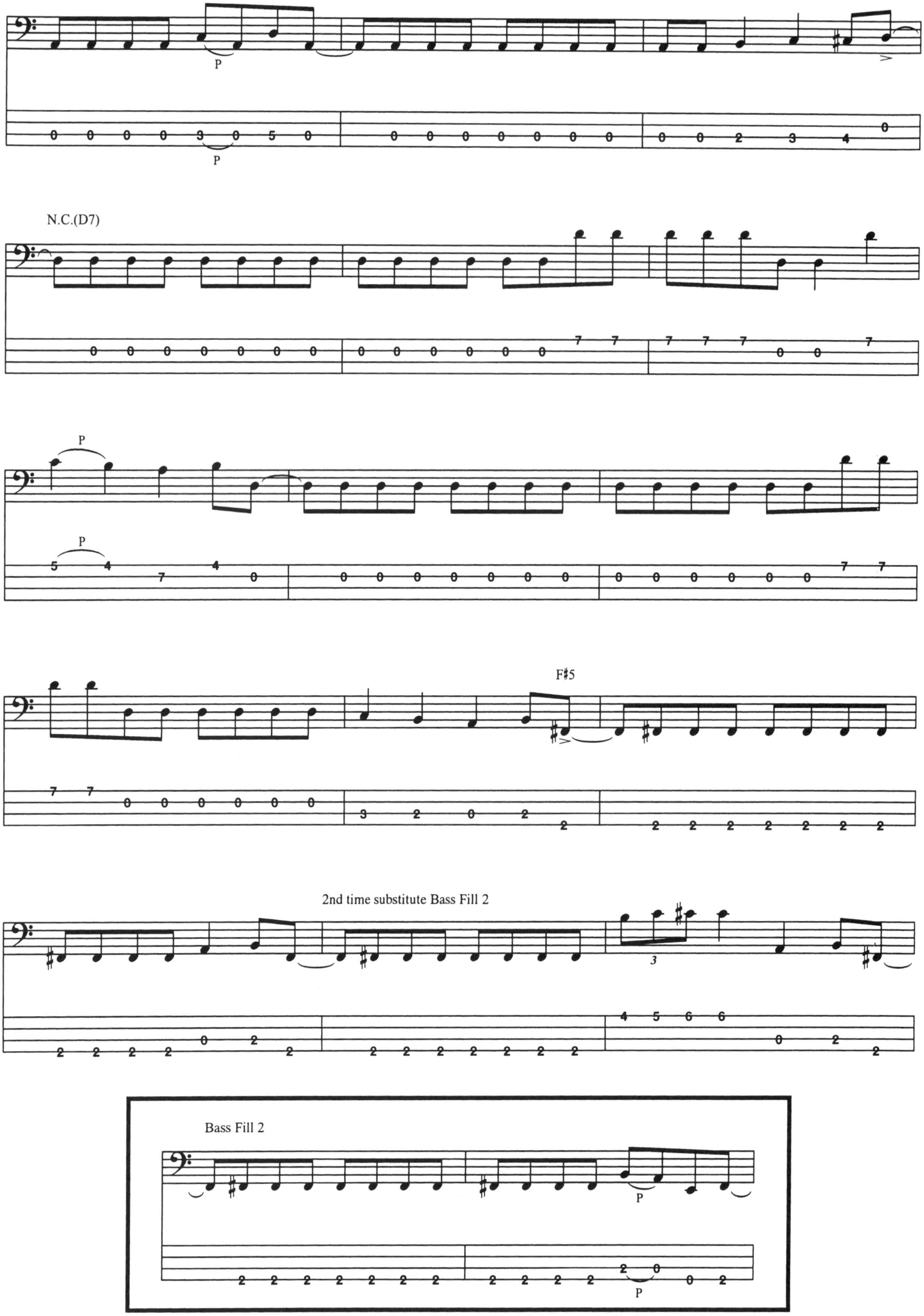
P
N.C.(D7)
F♯5
2nd time substitute Bass Fill 2
Bass Fill 2

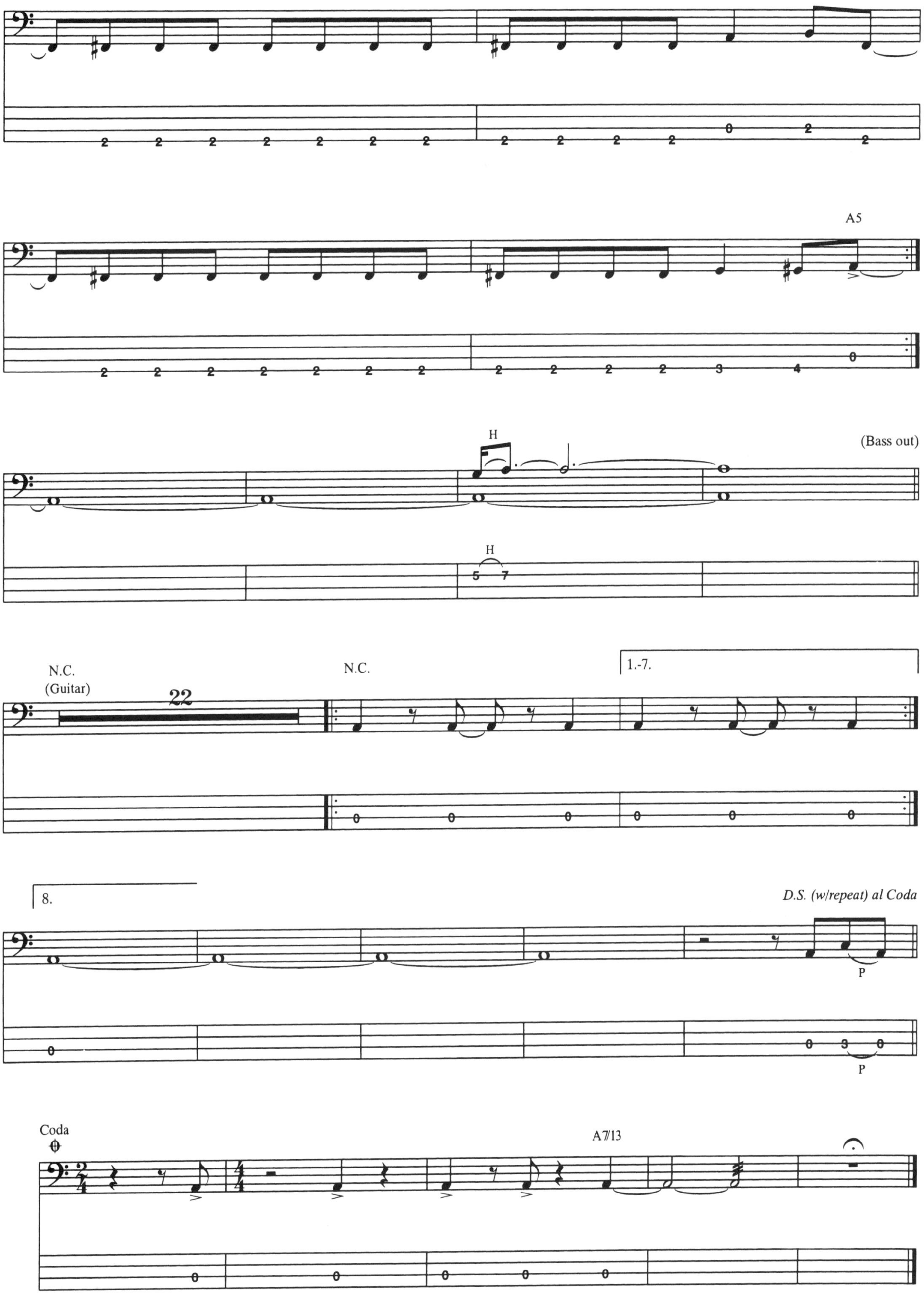
A5
H
(Bass out)
N.C.
(Guitar)
22
N.C.
1.-7.
8.
D.S. (w/repeat) al Coda
P
Coda
A7/13

THE STROKE

Words and Music by
Billy Squier

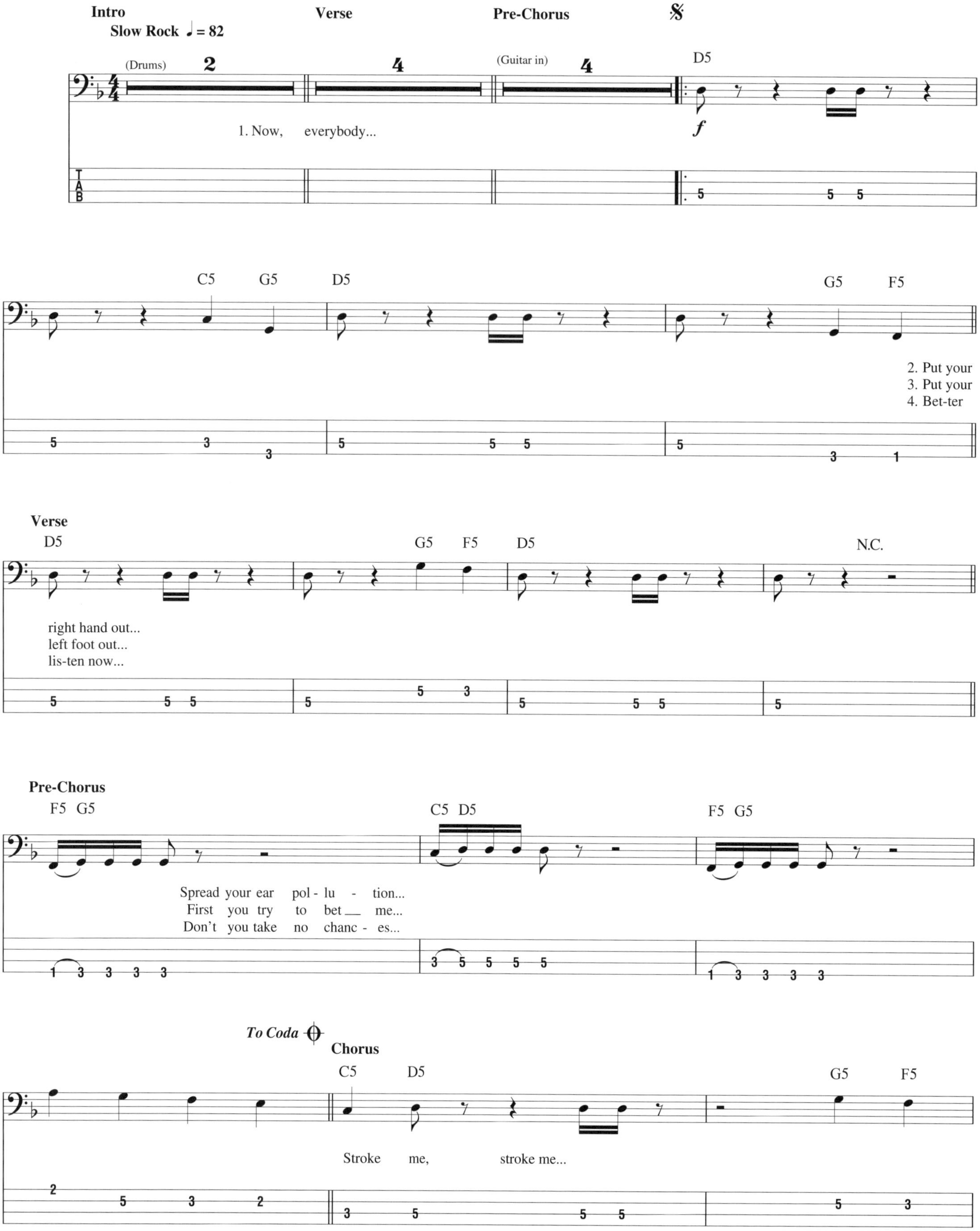

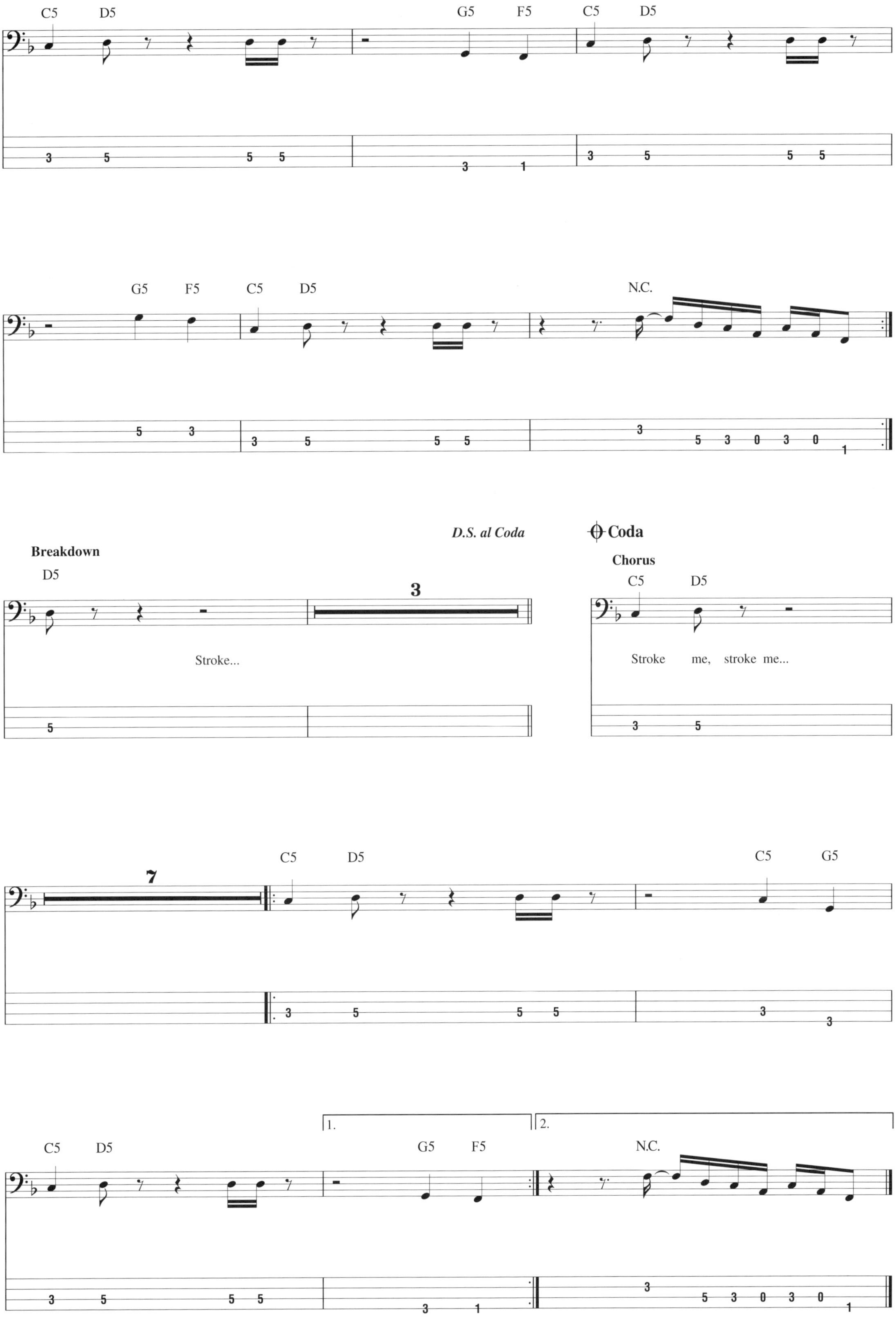
C5 D5 G5 F5 C5 D5
G5 F5 C5 D5 N.C.
Breakdown
D5
Stroke...
D.S. al Coda
Coda
Chorus
C5 D5
Stroke me, stroke me...
C5 D5 C5 G5
1.
2.
C5 D5 G5 F5 N.C.

SUNDAY PAPERS

Words and Music by
Joe Jackson

Chorus

Sun - day pa - pers...

Verse

2. Moth - er's wheel - chair stays out in the hall...

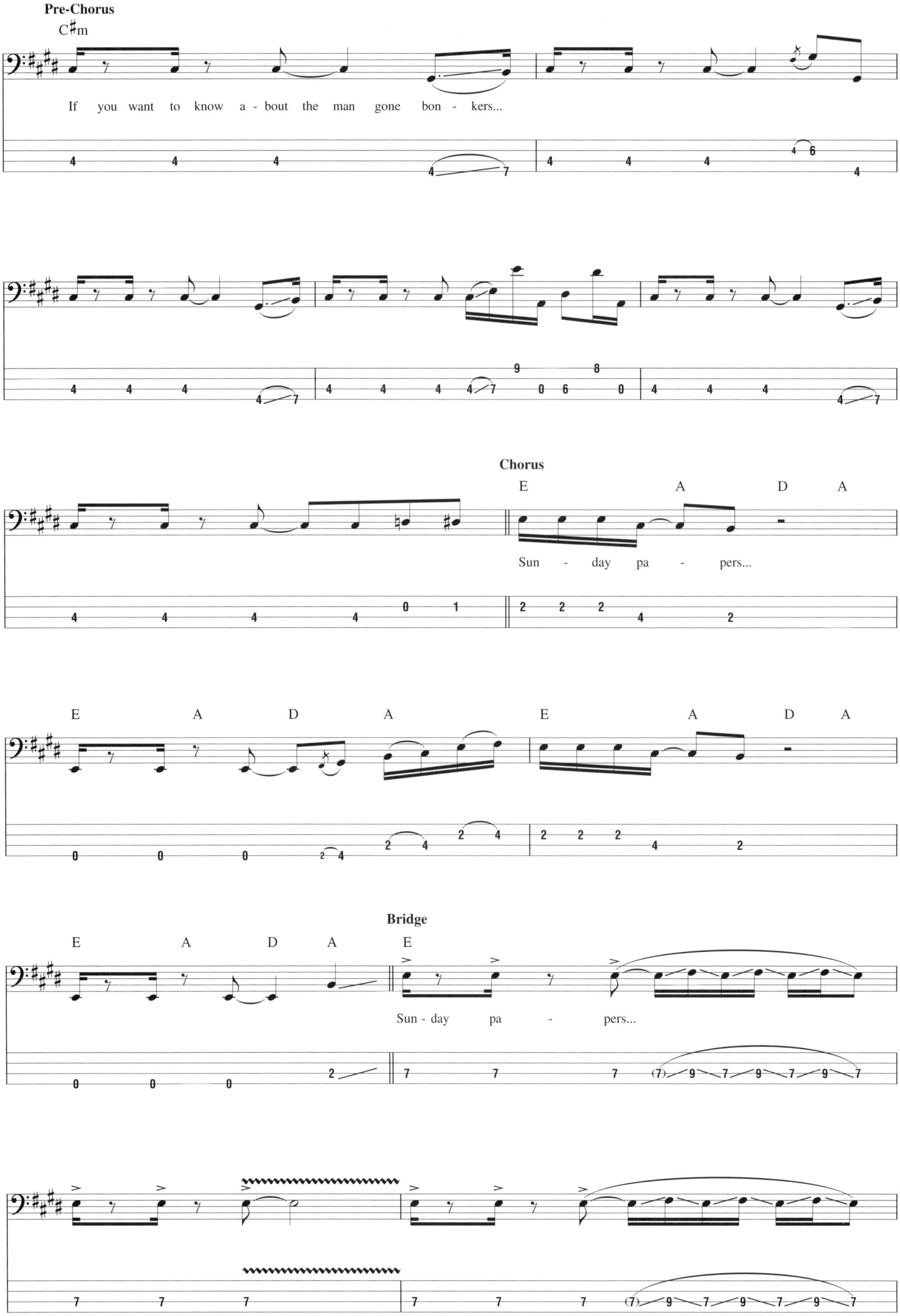
Pre-Chorus
C♯m
If you want to know a - bout the man gone bon - kers...
Chorus
E A D A
Sun - day pa - pers...
E A D A
E A D A
E A D A
Bridge
E
Sun - day pa - pers...

99

Pre-Chorus

If you want to know a - bout the gay pol - i - ti - cian...

Chorus

Sun - day pa - pers...

Bridge

Sun - day pa - pers...

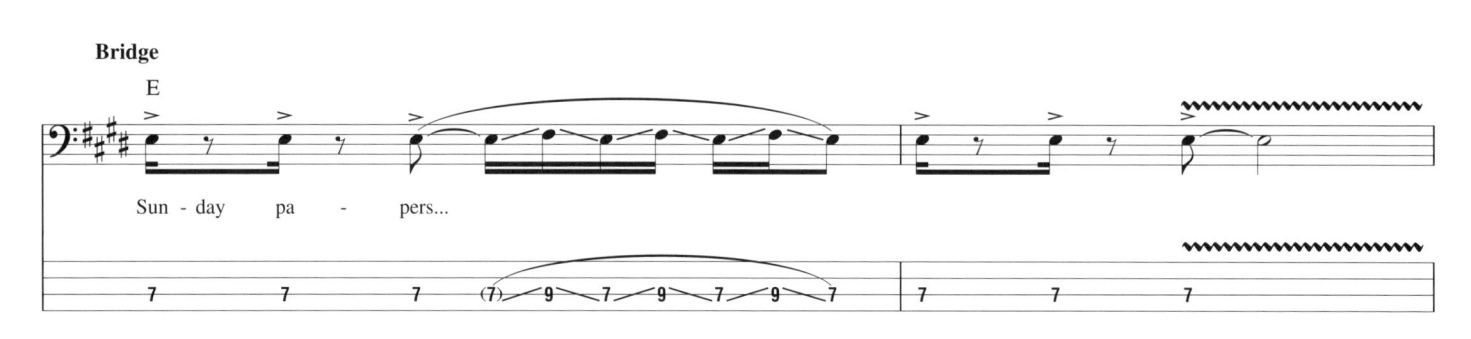

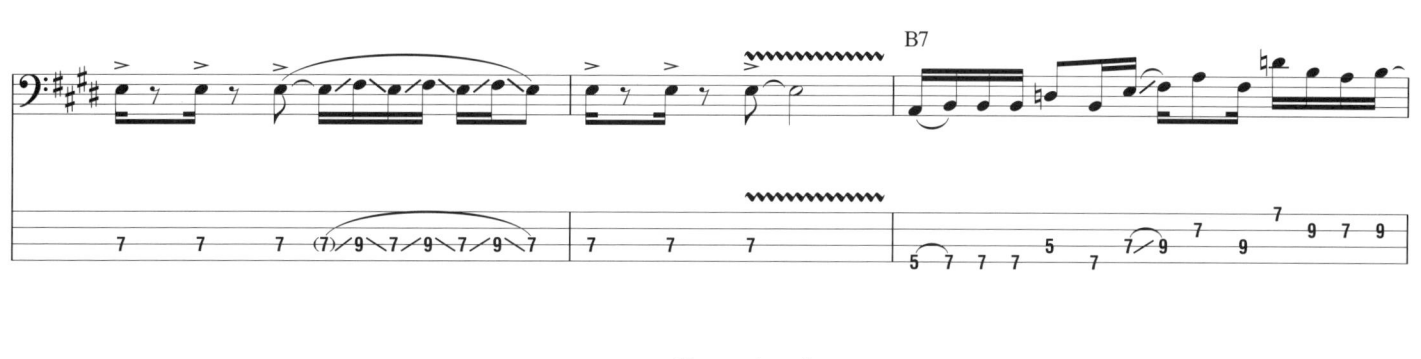

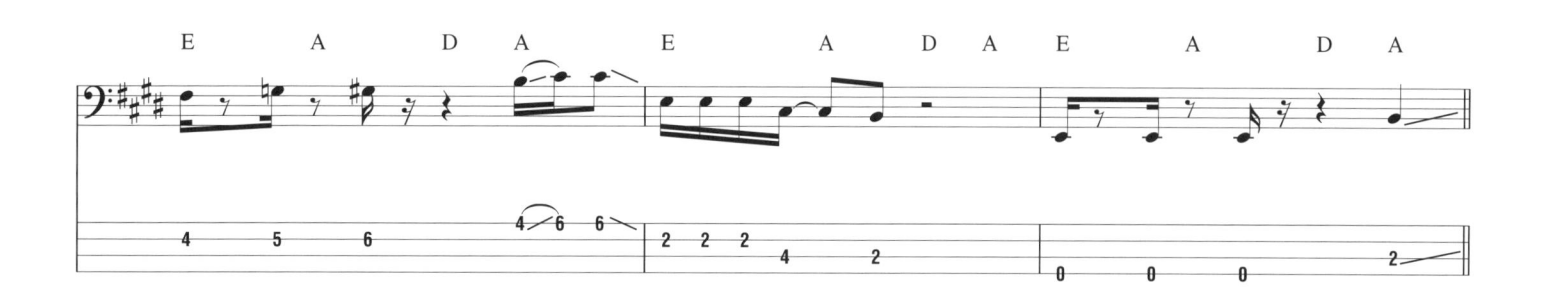

Harmonica solo

Bridge

Sun-day pa - pers...

Outro-Chorus

Sun-day pa - pers...

Double-time feel

Begin fade

Fade out

WELCOME TO THE JUNGLE

Words and Music by
W. Axl Rose, Slash,
Izzy Stradlin', Duff McKagan
and Steven Adler

Copyright © 1987 Guns N' Roses Music (ASCAP)
International Copyright Secured   All Rights Reserved

And when you're high ___ (etc.)

G F A G E
sl.
Guitar solo II
C♯5 B5 A5 B5 A5 B5 A5 B5 C5
2
C♯5 B5 A5 B5 A5 1/2 E5 B5
E5 B5
F♯5 E5 F♯5 E5 F♯5 E5 F♯5
B N.C.

F♯5 F5 F♯5 G5
A5 G♯5 A5 B♭5 C C/B C/A C/G D D/C♯ D/B D/A E5
In the jungle, welcome to the jungle, (etc.)
C C/B C/A C/G D D/C♯ D/B D/A E5
C C/B C/A C/G D D/C♯ D/B D/A E5
C C/B C/A C/G
D D/C♯ D/B D/A E5 D5 B♭5 A5 G5 E5 A G 1/2 E E7♯9
1/2

WHAT IS HIP

Words and Music by
Stephen Kupka, Emilio Castillo
and David Garibaldi

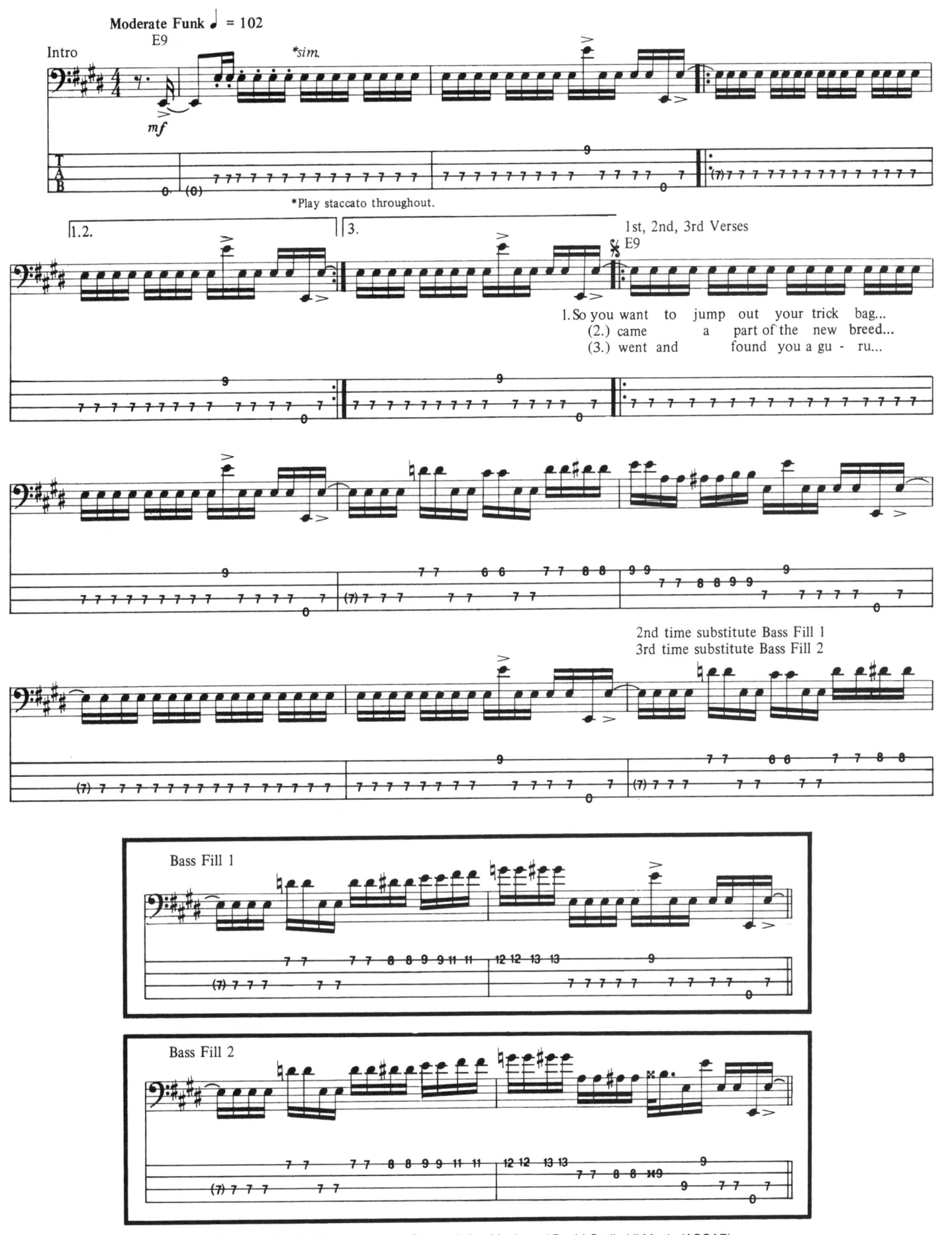

Chorus
E9
C9
sl.
What is hip?
Tell me, tell me...
(2nd time)
(2nd & 3rd times)
sl.
E9
B7+5
E9
(2nd time)
To Coda
F♯9
N.C.
G9
N.C.
G9
N.C.
G9
1.
N.C.
G9
F♯9
F9
E9
2.
N.C.
2. You be-
Bridge
A9
E9
A9
Hip - ness is...

109

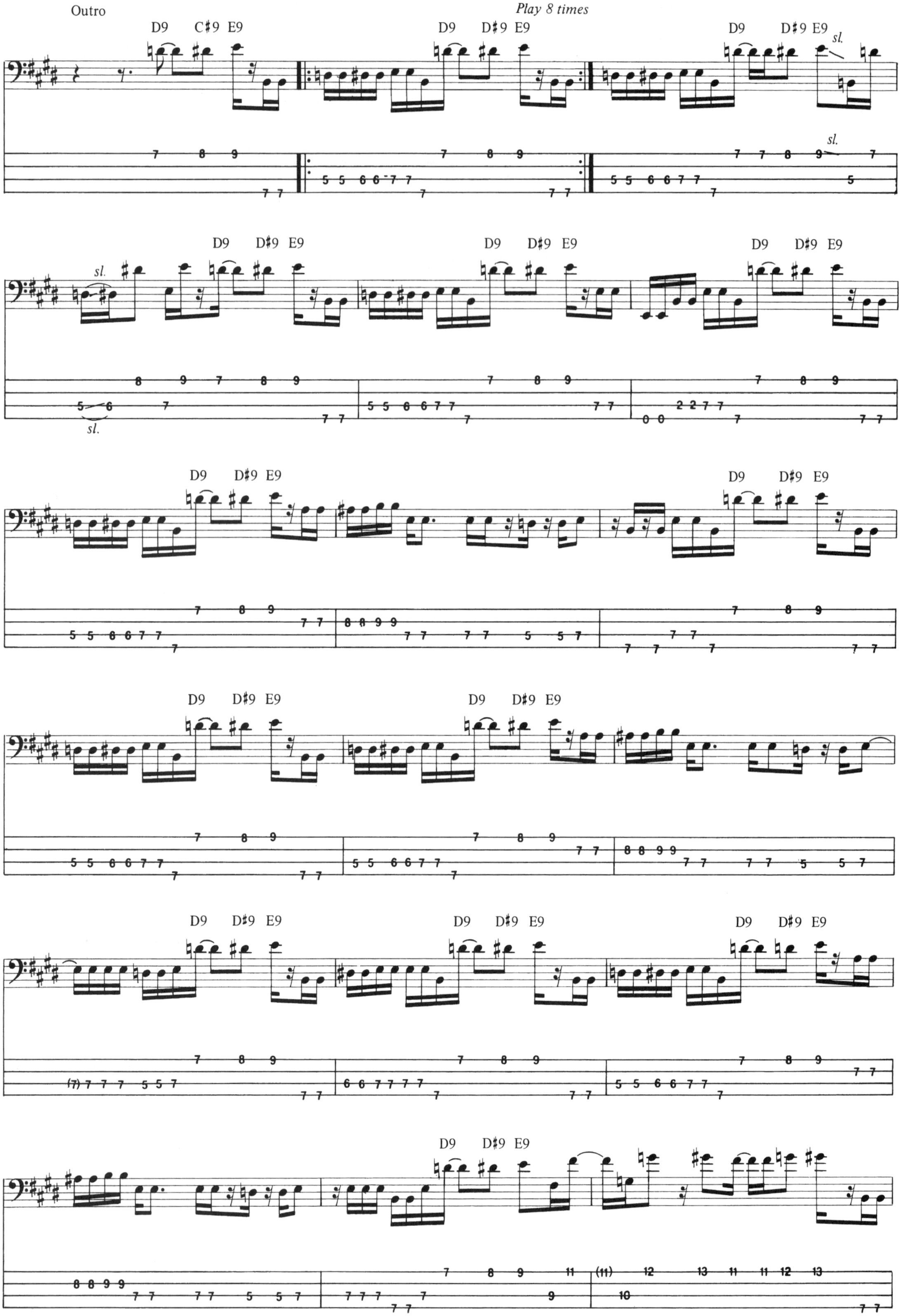
Outro
Play 8 times
D9 C♯9 E9
D9 D♯9 E9
sl.

D9 D♯9 E9
D9 D♯9 E9
D9 D♯9 E9
D9 D♯9 E9
D9 D♯9 E9
D♯9 D9 C♯9
D9 D♯9 E9
B7♯9
N.C.(E5)
sl.

YOU CAN CALL ME AL

Words and Music by
Paul Simon

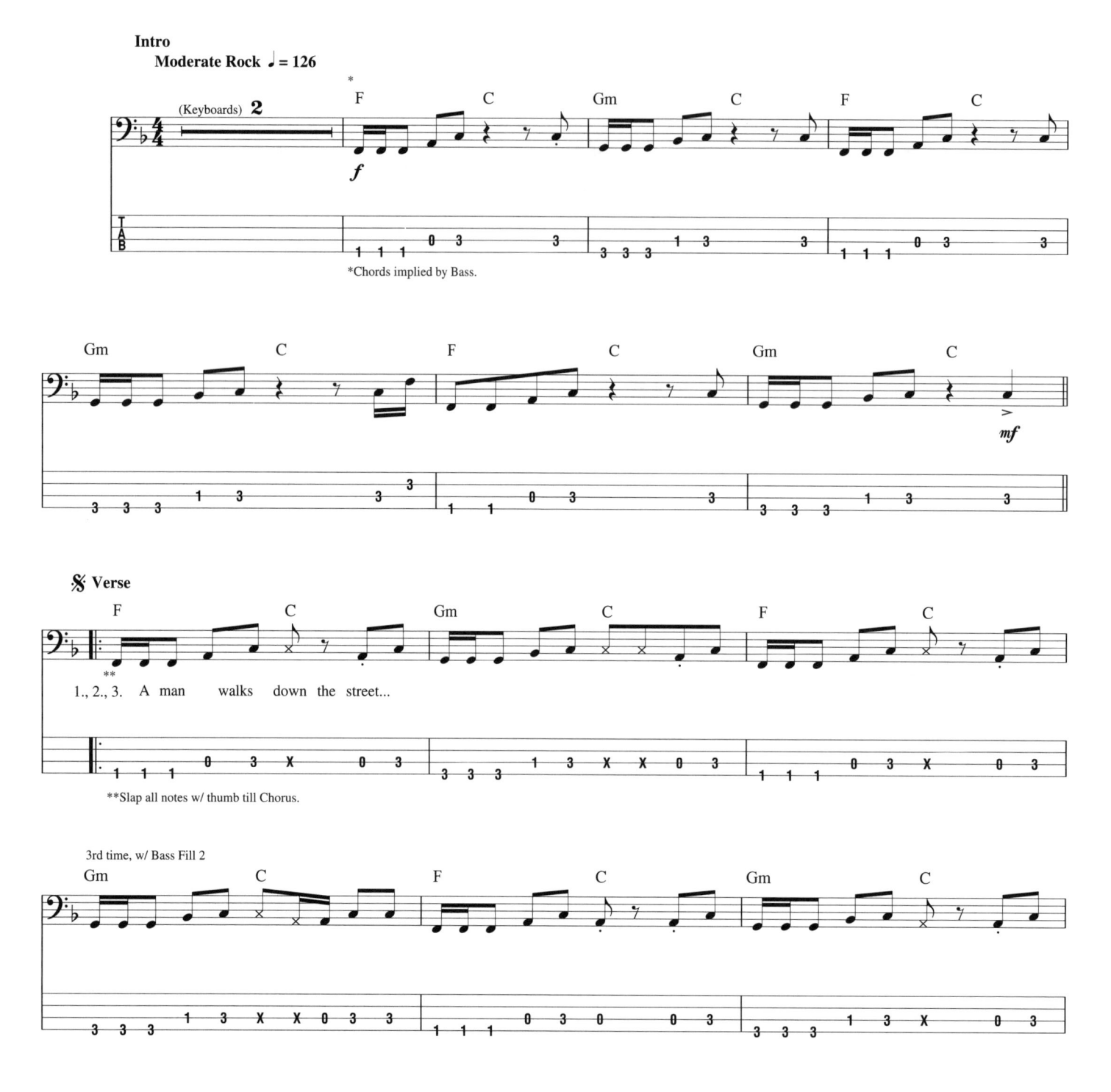

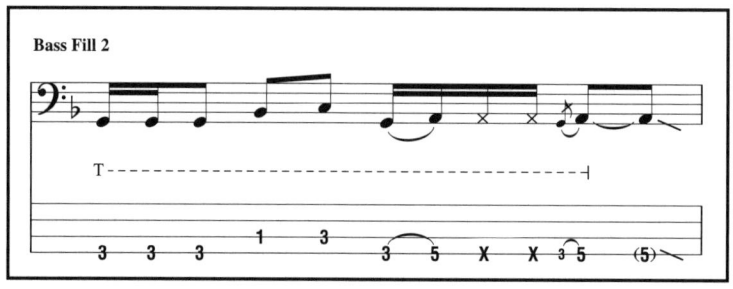

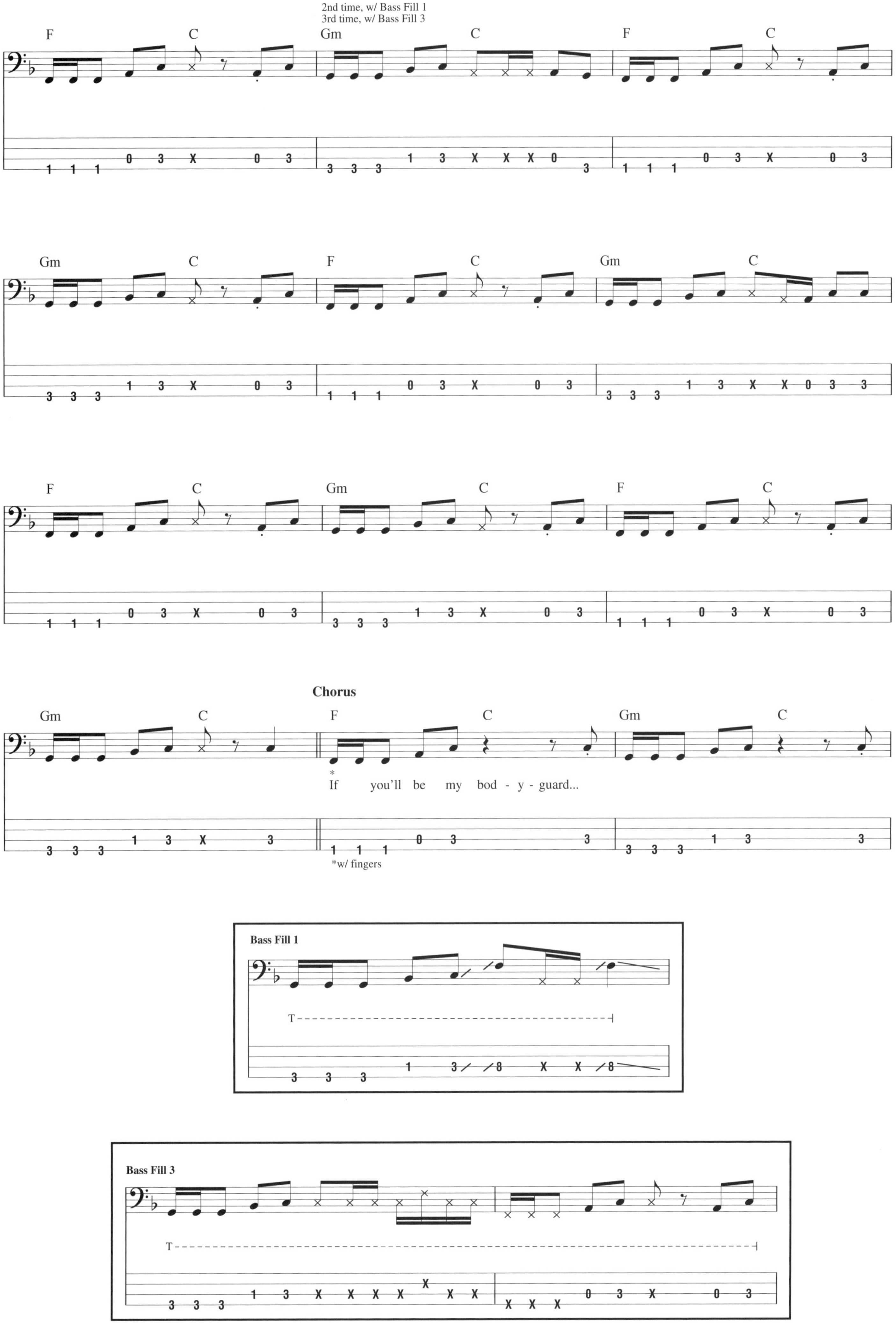
2nd time, w/ Bass Fill 1
3rd time, w/ Bass Fill 3
F C Gm C F C
Gm C F C Gm C
F C Gm C F C
Chorus
Gm C F C Gm C
*
If you'll be my bod - y - guard...
*w/ fingers
Bass Fill 1
T
Bass Fill 3
T

Penny Whistle Solo

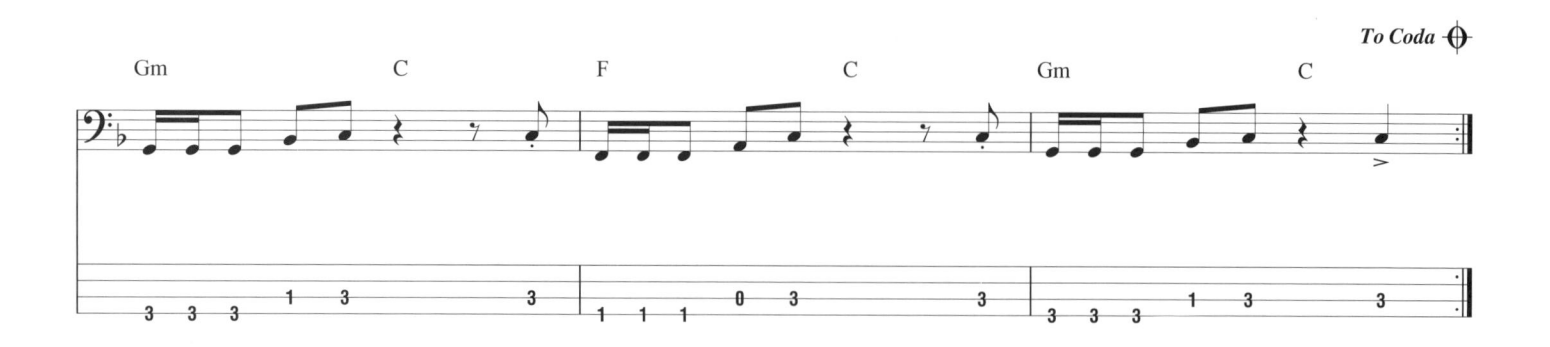

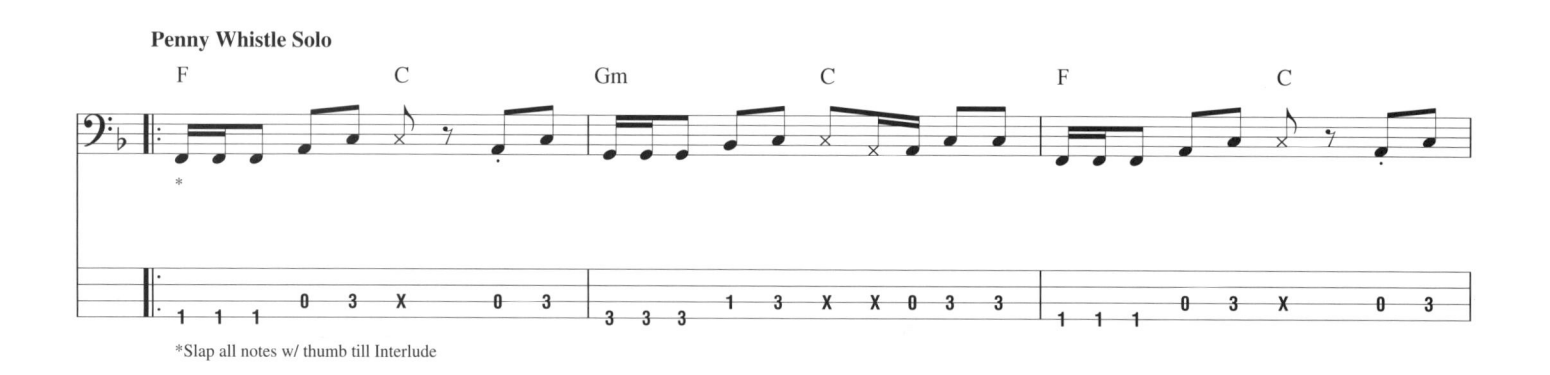

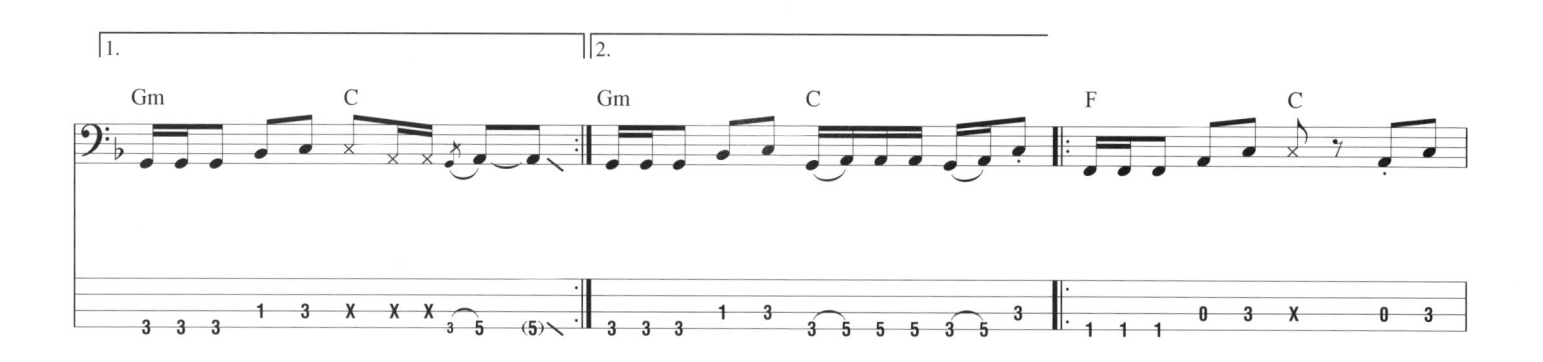

*Slap all notes w/ thumb till Interlude

114

2.
Interlude
Gm C F C Gm C
*w/ fingers
F C Gm C F C
D.S. al Coda
Gm C F C Gm C
Coda
F C Gm C F C
Na, na, na, na...
**Slap all notes w/ thumb till Bass Solo.
Gm C F C Gm C
F C Gm C F C

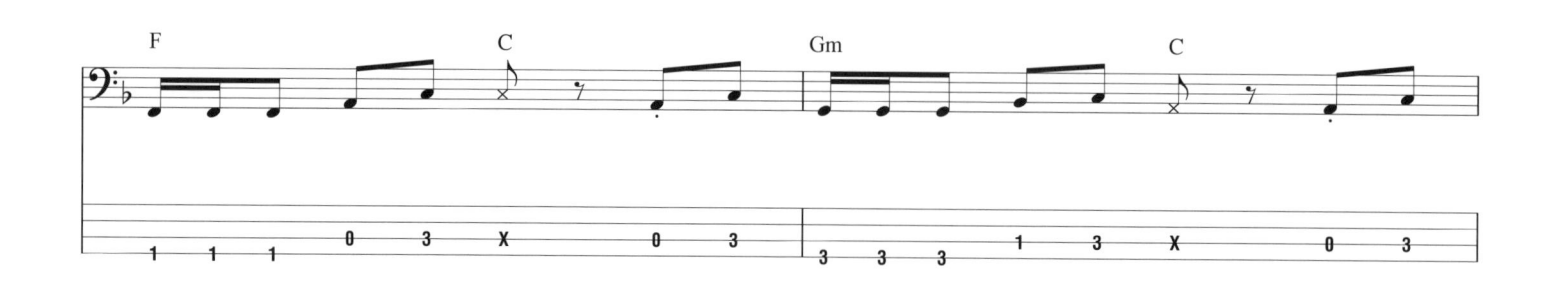

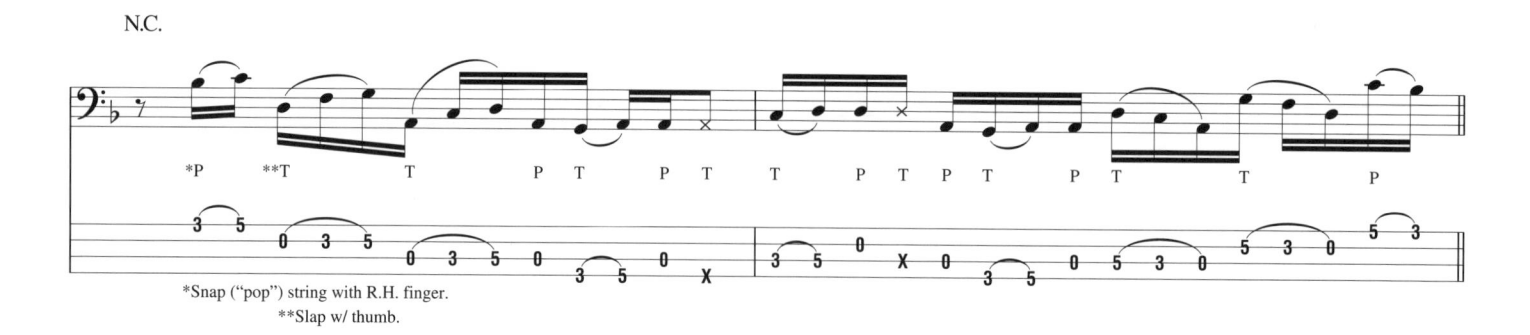

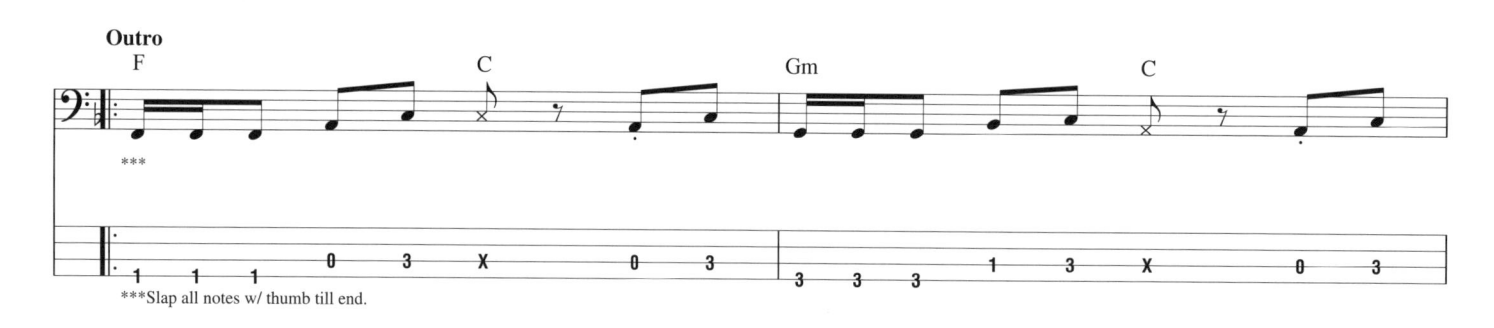

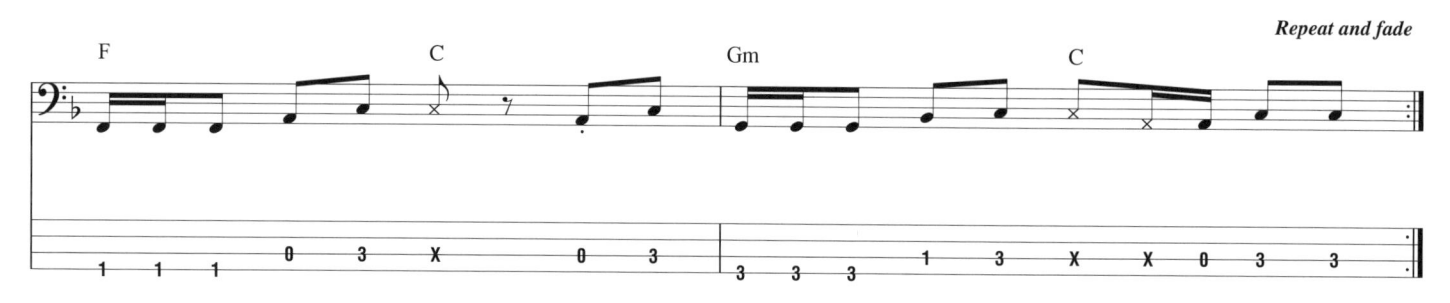

*Snap ("pop") string with R.H. finger.
**Slap w/ thumb.

Outro

***Slap all notes w/ thumb till end.

Repeat and fade

Bass Notation Legend

Bass music can be notated two different ways: on a *musical staff*, and in *tablature*.

THE MUSICAL STAFF shows pitches and rhythms and is divided by bar lines into measures. Pitches are named after the first seven letters of the alphabet.

TABLATURE graphically represents the bass fingerboard. Each horizontal line represents a string, and each number represents a fret.

HAMMER-ON: Strike the first (lower) note with one finger, then sound the higher note (on the same string) with another finger by fretting it without picking.

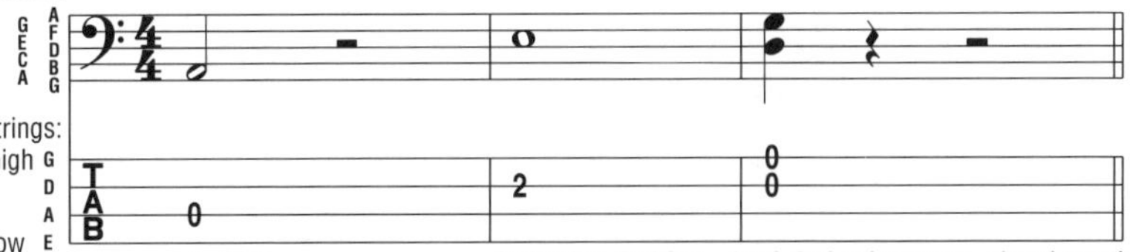

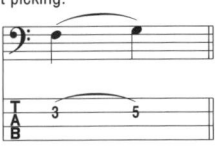

PULL-OFF: Place both fingers on the notes to be sounded. Strike the first note and without picking, pull the finger off to sound the second (lower) note.

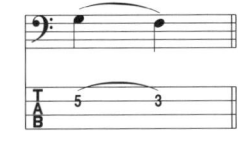

LEGATO SLIDE: Strike the first note and then slide the same fret-hand finger up or down to the second note. The second note is not struck.

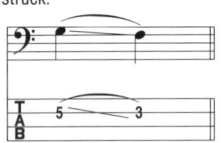

SHIFT SLIDE: Same as legato slide, except the second note is struck.

TRILL: Very rapidly alternate between the notes indicated by continuously hammering on and pulling off.

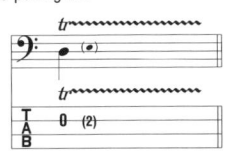

TREMOLO PICKING: The note is picked as rapidly and continuously as possible.

VIBRATO: The string is vibrated by rapidly bending and releasing the note with the fretting hand.

SHAKE: Using one finger, rapidly alternate between two notes on one string by sliding either a half-step above or below.

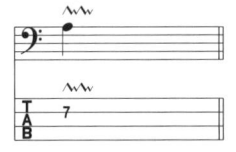

NATURAL HARMONIC: Strike the note while the fret hand lightly touches the string directly over the fret indicated.

MUFFLED STRINGS: A percussive sound is produced by laying the fret hand across the string(s) without depressing them and striking them with the pick hand.

BEND: Strike the note and bend up the interval shown.

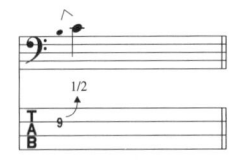

BEND AND RELEASE: Strike the note and bend up as indicated, then release back to the original note. Only the first note is struck.

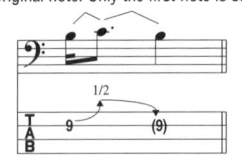

RIGHT-HAND TAP: Hammer ("tap") the fret indicated with the "pick-hand" index or middle finger and pull off to the note fretted by the fret hand.

LEFT-HAND TAP: Hammer ("tap") the fret indicated with the "fret-hand" index or middle finger.

SLAP: Strike ("slap") string with right-hand thumb.

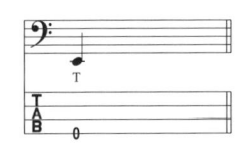

POP: Snap ("pop") string with right-hand index or middle finger.

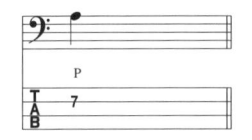

Additional Musical Definitions

- (accent) • Accentuate note (play it louder)
- (accent) • Accentuate note with great intensity 
- (staccato) • Play the note short 
- • Downstroke
- V • Upstroke

D.S. al Coda • Go back to the sign (𝄋), then play until the measure marked "*To Coda*," then skip to the section labelled "**Coda**."

NOTE: Tablature numbers in parentheses mean:
1. The note is being sustained over a system (note in standard notation is tied), or
2. The note is sustained, but a new articulation (such as a hammer-on, pull-off, slide or vibrato begins), or
3. The note is a barely audible "ghost" note (note in standard notation is also in parentheses).

D.C. al Fine • Go back to the beginning of the song and play until the measure marked "***Fine***" (end).

Bass Fig. • Label used to recall a recurring pattern.

Fill • Label used to identify a brief pattern which is to be inserted into the arrangement.

tacet • Instrument is silent (drops out).

• Repeat measures between signs.

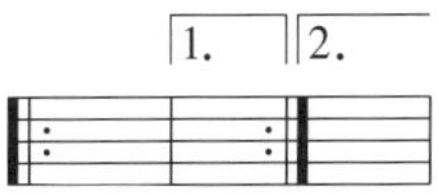

• When a repeated section has different endings, play the first ending only the first time and the second ending only the second time.

CHERRY LANE MUSIC COMPANY

6 East 32nd Street, New York, NY 10016

Quality in Printed Music

Guitar one
The Magazine You Can Play

Visit the Guitar One web site at **www.guitarone.com**

REFERENCE/INSTRUCTION

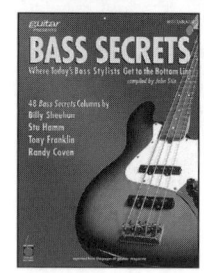

ACOUSTIC INSTRUMENTALISTS
INCLUDES TAB

Over 15 transcriptions from legendary artists such as Leo Kottke, John Fahey, Jorma Kaukonen, Chet Atkins, Adrian Legg, Jeff Beck, and more.

02500399 Play-It-Like-It-Is Guitar..............................$9.95

THE BEST BASS LINES
INCLUDES TAB

24 super songs: Bohemian Rhapsody • Celebrity Skin • Crash Into Me • Crazy Train • Glycerine • Money • November Rain • Smoke on the Water • Sweet Child O' Mine • What Would You Say • You're My Flavor • and more.

02500311 Play-It-Like-It-Is Bass $14.95

BLUES TAB
INCLUDES TAB

14 songs: Boom Boom • Cold Shot • Hide Away • I Can't Quit You Baby • I'm Your Hoochie Coochie Man • In 2 Deep • It Hurts Me Too • Talk to Your Daughter • The Thrill Is Gone • and more.

02500410 Play-It-Like-It-Is Guitar...........................$14.95

CLASSIC ROCK TAB
INCLUDES TAB

15 rock hits: Cat Scratch Fever • Crazy Train • Day Tripper • Hey Joe • Hot Blooded • Start Me Up • We Will Rock You • You Really Got Me • and more.

02500408 Play-It-Like-It-Is Guitar...........................$14.95

MODERN ROCK TAB
INCLUDES TAB

15 of modern rock's best: Are You Gonna Go My Way • Denial • Hanging by a Moment • I Did It • My Hero • Nobody's Real • Rock the Party (Off the Hook) • Shock the Monkey • Slide • Spit It Out • and more.

02500409 Play-It-Like-It-Is Guitar...........................$14.95

SIGNATURE SONGS
INCLUDES TAB

21 artists' trademark hits: Crazy Train (Ozzy Osbourne) • My Generation (The Who) • Smooth (Santana) • Sunshine of Your Love (Cream) • Walk This Way (Aerosmith) • Welcome to the Jungle (Guns N' Roses) • What Would You Say (Dave Matthews Band) • and more.

02500303 Play-It-Like-It-Is Guitar...........................$16.95

BASS SECRETS
WHERE TODAY'S BASS STYLISTS GET TO THE BOTTOM LINE
compiled by John Stix

Bass Secrets brings together 48 columns highlighting specific topics – ranging from the technical to the philosophical – from masters such as Stu Hamm, Randy Coven, Tony Franklin and Billy Sheehan. They cover topics including tapping, walking bass lines, soloing, hand positions, harmonics and more. Clearly illustrated with musical examples.

02500100 ....$12.95

CLASSICS ILLUSTRATED
WHERE BACH MEETS ROCK
by Robert Phillips

Classics Illustrated is designed to demonstrate for readers and players the links between rock and classical music. Each of the 30 columns from *Guitar* highlights one musical concept and provides clear examples in both styles of music. This cool book lets you study moving bass lines over stationary chords in the music of Bach and Guns N' Roses, learn the similarities between "Leyenda" and "Diary of a Madman," and much more!

02500101 ....$9.95

GUITAR SECRETS
INCLUDES TAB
WHERE ROCK'S GUITAR MASTERS SHARE THEIR TRICKS, TIPS & TECHNIQUES
compiled by John Stix

This unique and informative compilation features 42 columns culled from *Guitar* magazine. Readers will discover dozens of techniques and playing tips, and gain practical advice and words of wisdom from guitar masters.

02500099 ....$10.95

IN THE LISTENING ROOM
WHERE ARTISTS CRITIQUE THE MUSIC OF THEIR PEERS
compiled by John Stix

A compilation of 75 columns from *Guitar* magazine, *In the Listening Room* provides a unique opportunity for readers to hear major recording artists remark on the music of their peers. These artists were given no information about what they would hear, and their comments often tell as much about themselves as they do about the music they listened to. Includes candid critiques by music legends like Aerosmith, Jeff Beck, Jack Bruce, Dimebag Darrell, Buddy Guy, Kirk Hammett, Eric Johnson, John McLaughlin, Dave Navarro, Carlos Santana, Joe Satriani, Stevie Ray Vaughan, and many others.

02500097 ....$14.95

LEGENDS OF LEAD GUITAR
THE BEST OF INTERVIEWS: 1995-2000

This is a fascinating compilation of interviews with today's greatest guitarists! From deeply rooted blues giants to the most fearless pioneers, legendary players reveal how they achieve their extraordinary craft.

02500329 ....$14.95

LESSON LAB

This exceptional book/CD pack features more than 20 in-depth lessons. Tackle in detail a variety of pertinent music- and guitar-related subjects, such as scales, chords, theory, guitar technique, songwriting, and much more!

02500330 Book/CD Pack..$19.95

NOISE & FEEDBACK

THE BEST OF 1995-2000: YOUR QUESTIONS ANSWERED

If you ever wanted to know about a specific guitar lick, trick, technique or effect, this book/CD pack is for you! It features over 70 lessons on composing • computer assistance • education and career advice • equipment • technique • terminology and notation • tunings • and more.

02500328 Book/CD Pack..$17.95

OPEN EARS
A JOURNEY THROUGH LIFE WITH GUITAR IN HAND
by Steve Morse

In this collection of 50 *Guitar* magazine columns from the mid-'90s on, guitarist Steve Morse sets the story straight about what being a working musician *really* means. He deals out practical advice on: playing with the band, songwriting, recording and equipment, and more, through anecdotes of his hard-knock lessons learned.

02500333 ....$10.95

SPOTLIGHT ON STYLE

THE BEST OF 1995-2000: AN EXPLORER'S GUIDE TO GUITAR

This book and CD cover 18 of the world's most popular guitar styles, including: blues guitar • classical guitar • country guitar • funk guitar • jazz guitar • Latin guitar • metal • rockabilly and more!

02500320 Book/CD Pack..$19.95

STUDIO CITY
PROFESSIONAL SESSION RECORDING FOR GUITARISTS
by Carl Verheyen

In this collection of columns from *Guitar Magazine*, guitarists will learn how to: exercise studio etiquette and act professionally • acquire, assemble and set up gear for sessions • use the tricks of the trade to become a studio hero • get repeat call-backs • and more.

02500195 ....$9.95

EXCLUSIVELY DISTRIBUTED BY

HAL•LEONARD® CORPORATION

7777 W. BLUEMOUND RD. P.O. BOX 13819 MILWAUKEE, WI 53213

Visit Cherry Lane online at **www.cherrylane.com**

METALLICA

Visit Cherry Lane Online at
www.cherrylane.com

Prices, contents and availability subject to change without notice.

MATCHING FOLIOS

...AND JUSTICE FOR ALL
02506965	Play-It-Like-It-Is Guitar	$22.95
02506982	Play-It-Like-It-Is Bass	$19.95
02506856	Easy Guitar	$12.95
02503504	Drums	$18.95

GARAGE INC.
02500070	Play-It-Like-It-Is Guitar	$24.95
02500075	Play-It-Like-It-Is Bass	$24.95
02500076	Easy Guitar	$14.95
02500077	Drums	$18.95

KILL 'EM ALL
02507018	Play-It-Like-It-Is Guitar	$19.95
02507039	Play-It-Like-It-Is Bass	$19.95
02506860	Easy Guitar	$12.95
02503508	Play-It-Like-It-Is Drums	$18.95

LIVE: BINGE AND PURGE
02501232	Play-It-Like-It-Is Guitar	$19.95

LOAD
02501275	Play-It-Like-It-Is-Guitar	$24.95
02505919	Play-It-Like-It-Is-Bass	$19.95
02506881	Easy Guitar	$15.95
02503515	Drums	$18.95

MASTER OF PUPPETS
02507920	Play-It-Like-It-Is Guitar	$19.95
02506961	Play-It-Like-It-Is Bass	$19.95
02506859	Easy Guitar	$12.95
02503502	Drums	$18.95

METALLICA
02501195	Play-It-Like-It-Is Guitar	$22.95
02505911	Play-It-Like-It-Is Bass	$19.95
02506869	Easy Guitar	$14.95
02503509	Drums	$18.95

RE-LOAD
02501297	Play-It-Like-It-Is Guitar	$24.95
02505926	Play-It-Like-It-Is Bass	$21.95
02506887	Easy Guitar	$15.95
02503517	Drums	$18.95

RIDE THE LIGHTNING
02507019	Play-It-Like-It-Is Guitar	$19.95
02507040	Play-It-Like-It-Is Bass	$17.95
02506861	Easy Guitar	$12.95
02503507	Drums	$17.95

S&M HIGHLIGHTS
02500279	Play-It-Like-It-Is Guitar	$24.95
02500288	Play-It-Like-It-Is Bass	$19.95

COLLECTIONS

BEST OF METALLICA
02500424	Transcribed Full Scores	$24.95

BEST OF METALLICA
02502204	P/V/G	$17.95

5 OF THE BEST
02506210	Play-It-Like-It-Is Guitar – Vol. 1	$12.95
02506235	Play-It-Like-It-Is Guitar – Vol. 2	$12.95

LEGENDARY LICKS
An Inside Look at the Styles of Metallica
Book/CD Packs
02500181	Guitar 1983-1988	$22.95
02500182	Guitar 1988-1996	$22.95
02500180	Bass Legendary Licks	$19.95
02500172	Drum Legendary Licks	$19.95

LEGENDARY LICKS DVDs
A Step-by-Step Breakdown of Metallica's Styles and Techniques
02500479	Guitar 1983-1988	$24.95
02500480	Guitar 1988-1997	$24.95
02500481	Bass 1983-1988	$24.95
02500484	Bass 1988-1997	$24.95
02500482	Drums 1983-1988	$24.95
02500485	Drums 1988-1997	$24.95

RIFF BY RIFF
02506313	Guitar – Riff by Riff	$19.95

INSTRUCTION

METALLICA WITH EASY GUITAR WITH LESSONS, VOLUME 1
02506877	Easy Recorded Versions	$14.95

METALLICA – EASY GUITAR WITH LESSONS, VOLUME 2
02500419	Easy Guitar	$14.95

LEARN TO PLAY WITH METALLICA
Book/CD Packs
02500138	Guitar	$12.95
02500189	Bass	$12.95
02500190	Drums	$12.95

PLAYERS

THE ART OF KIRK HAMMETT
02506325	Guitar Transcriptions	$17.95

THE ART OF JAMES HETFIELD
02500016	Guitar Transcriptions	$17.95

REFERENCE

METALLICA – THE COMPLETE LYRICS
02500478	Lyrics	$19.95

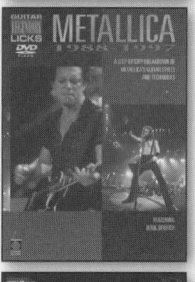

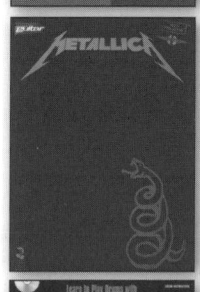

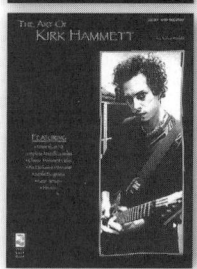

CHERRY LANE MUSIC COMPANY
6 East 32nd Street, New York, NY 10016
Quality in Printed Music

Exclusively Distributed By
HAL•LEONARD CORPORATION
7777 W. Bluemound Rd. P.O. Box 13819 Milwaukee, WI 53213

THE HOTTEST TAB SONGBOOKS AVAILABLE FOR GUITAR & BASS!

PLAY IT LIKE IT IS GUITAR WITH TABLATURE — NOTE-FOR-NOTE TRANSCRIPTIONS

PLAY IT LIKE IT IS BASS WITH TABLATURE — NOTE-FOR-NOTE TRANSCRIPTIONS

from **CHERRY LANE MUSIC COMPANY** — *Quality in Printed Music*

Guitar Transcriptions

Code	Title	Price
02500593	Best of Ryan Adams	$19.95
02500443	Alien Ant Farm – ANThology	$19.95
02501272	Bush – 16 Stone	$21.95
02500193	Bush – The Science of Things	$19.95
02500098	Coal Chamber	$19.95
02500174	Coal Chamber – Chamber Music	$19.95
02500179	Mary Chapin Carpenter – Authentic Guitar Style of	$16.95
02500132	Evolution of Fear Factory	$19.95
02500198	Best of Foreigner	$19.95
02501242	Guns N' Roses – Anthology	$24.95
02506953	Guns N' Roses – Appetite for Destruction	$22.95
02501286	Guns N' Roses Complete, Volume 1	$24.95
02501287	Guns N' Roses Complete, Volume 2	$24.95
02506211	Guns N' Roses – 5 of the Best, Vol. 1	$12.95
02506975	Guns N' Roses – GN'R Lies	$19.95
02500299	Guns N' Roses – Live Era '87-'93 Highlights	$24.95
02501193	Guns N' Roses – Use Your Illusion I	$24.95
02501194	Guns N' Roses – Use Your Illusion II	$24.95
02500458	Best of Warren Haynes	$19.95
02500387	Best of Heart	$19.95
02500007	Hole – Celebrity Skin	$19.95
02501260	Hole – Live Through This	$19.95
02500516	Jimmy Eat World	$19.95
02500554	Jack Johnson – Brushfire Fairytales	$19.95
02500380	Lenny Kravitz – Greatest Hits	$19.95
02500469	Lenny Kravitz – Lenny	$19.95
02500024	Best of Lenny Kravitz	$19.95
02500375	Lifehouse – No Name Face	$19.95
02500558	Lifehouse – Stanley Climbfall	$19.95
02500362	Best of Little Feat	$19.95
02501259	Machine Head – Burn My Eyes	$19.95
02501173	Machine Head – The Burning Red	$19.95
02500305	Best of The Marshall Tucker Band	$19.95
02501357	Dave Matthews Band – Before These Crowded Streets	$19.95
02500553	Dave Matthews Band – Busted Stuff	$22.95
02501279	Dave Matthews Band – Crash	$19.95
02500389	Dave Matthews Band – Everyday	$19.95
02500488	Dave Matthews Band – Live in Chicago 12/19/98 at the United Center, Vol. 1	$19.95
02500489	Dave Matthews Band – Live in Chicago 12/19/98 at the United Center, Vol. 2	$19.95
02501266	Dave Matthews Band – Under the Table and Dreaming	$19.95
02500131	Dave Matthews/Tim Reynolds – Live at Luther College, Vol. 1	$19.95
02500611	Dave Matthews/Tim Reynolds – Live at Luther College, Vol. 2	$19.95
02500529	John Mayer – Room for Squares	$19.95
02506965	Metallica – …And Justice for All	$22.95
02506210	Metallica – 5 of the Best/Vol.1	$12.95
02506235	Metallica – 5 of the Best/Vol. 2	$12.95
02500070	Metallica – Garage, Inc.	$24.95
02507018	Metallica – Kill 'Em All	$19.95
02501232	Metallica – Live: Binge & Purge	$19.95
02501275	Metallica – Load	$24.95
02507920	Metallica – Master of Puppets	$19.95
02501195	Metallica – Metallica	$22.95
02501297	Metallica – ReLoad	$24.95
02507019	Metallica – Ride the Lightning	$19.95
02500279	Metallica – S&M Highlights	$24.95
02500577	Molly Hatchet – 5 of the Best	$9.95
02501353	Best of Steve Morse	$19.95
02500448	Best of Ted Nugent	$19.95
02500348	Ozzy Osbourne – Blizzard of Ozz	$19.95
02501277	Ozzy Osbourne – Diary of a Madman	$19.95
02509973	Ozzy Osbourne – Songbook	$24.95
02507904	Ozzy Osbourne/Randy Rhoads Tribute	$22.95
02500316	Papa Roach – Infest	$19.95
02500545	Papa Roach – Lovehatetragedy	$19.95
02500194	Powerman 5000 – Tonight the Stars Revolt!	$17.95
02500025	Primus Anthology – A-N (Guitar/Bass)	$19.95
02500091	Primus Anthology – O-Z (Guitar/Bass)	$19.95
02500468	Primus – Sailing the Seas of Cheese	$19.95
02500508	Bonnie Raitt – Silver Lining	$19.95
02501268	Joe Satriani	$22.95
02501299	Joe Satriani – Crystal Planet	$24.95
02500306	Joe Satriani – Engines of Creation	$22.95
02501205	Joe Satriani – The Extremist	$22.95
02507029	Joe Satriani – Flying in a Blue Dream	$22.95
02507074	Joe Satriani – Not of This Earth	$19.95
02500544	Joe Satriani – Strange Beautiful Music	$19.95
02506959	Joe Satriani – Surfing with the Alien	$19.95
02501226	Joe Satriani – Time Machine 1	$19.95
02500560	Joe Satriani Anthology	$24.95
02501255	Best of Joe Satriani	$19.95
02500088	Sepultura – Against	$19.95
02501239	Sepultura – Arise	$19.95
02501240	Sepultura – Beneath the Remains	$19.95
02501238	Sepultura – Chaos A.D.	$19.95
02500188	Best of the Brian Setzer Orchestra	$19.95
02500177	Sevendust	$19.95
02500176	Sevendust – Home	$19.95
02500090	Soulfly	$19.95
02501230	Soundgarden – Superunknown	$19.95
02501250	Best of Soundgarden	$19.95
02500168	Steely Dan's Greatest Songs	$19.95
02500167	Best of Steely Dan for Guitar	$19.95
02501263	Tesla – Time's Making Changes	$19.95
02500583	The White Stripes – White Blood Cells	$19.95
02500431	Best of Johnny Winter	$19.95
02500199	Best of Zakk Wylde	$22.95
02500517	WWE – Forceable Entry	$19.95
02500104	WWF: The Music, Vol.3	$19.95

Bass Transcriptions

Code	Title	Price
02500008	Best of Bush	$16.95
02500920	Bush – 16 Stone	$19.95
02506966	Guns N' Roses – Appetite for Destruction	$19.95
02500504	Best of Guns N' Roses for Bass	$14.95
02500013	Best of The Dave Matthews Band	$17.95
02505911	Metallica – Metallica	$19.95
02506982	Metallica – …And Justice for All	$19.95
02500075	Metallica – Garage, Inc.	$24.95
02507039	Metallica – Kill 'Em All	$19.95
02505919	Metallica – Load	$19.95
02506961	Metallica – Master of Puppets	$19.95
02505926	Metallica – ReLoad	$21.95
02507040	Metallica – Ride the Lightning	$17.95
02500288	Metallica – S&M Highlights	$19.95
02500347	Papa Roach – Infest	$17.95
02500539	Sittin' In with Rocco Prestia of Tower of Power	$19.95
02500025	Primus Anthology – A-N (Guitar/Bass)	$19.95
02500091	Primus Anthology – O-Z (Guitar/Bass)	$19.95
02500500	Best of Joe Satriani for Bass	$14.95
02500317	Victor Wooten Songbook	$19.95

Transcribed Scores

Code	Title	Price
02500361	Guns N' Roses Greatest Hits	$24.95
02500282	Lenny Kravitz – Greatest Hits	$24.95
02500496	Lenny Kravitz – Lenny	$24.95
02500424	Best of Metallica	$24.95
02500283	Joe Satriani – Greatest Hits	$24.95

For More Information, See Your Local Music Dealer, Or Write To:

HAL•LEONARD® CORPORATION
7777 W. BLUEMOUND RD. P.O. BOX 13819 MILWAUKEE, WI 53213

Prices, contents and availability subject to change without notice.

0303